CHICKASAWS AND CHOCTAWS

A Pamphlet of Information Concerning their History, Treaties, Government, Country, Laws, Politics and Affairs.

PRICE FIFTY CENTS

SR Scholarly Resources Inc.
1508 Pennsylvania Avenue · Wilmington, Delaware 19806

SCHOLARLY RESOURCES, INC.
Wilmington, Delaware • London

Reprint edition published in 1975

Library of Congress Catalog Card Number: 75-3678
ISBN: 0-8420-1844-1

Manufactured in the United States of America

CHICKASAWS AND CHOCTAWS

A Pamphlet of Information Concerning their History, Treaties, Government, Country, Laws, Politics and Affairs.

PRICE FIFTY CENTS

CHICKASAWS AND CHOCTAWS.

COMPRISING THE

TREATIES OF 1855 AND 1866.

THE OKLAHOMA BILL.

AND MANY LAWS OF ESPECIAL INTEREST TO NON-CITIZENS,

SUCH AS

THE PERMIT LAW,

THE LICENSED TRADER LAW,

THE STOCK LAW,

THE MINING LAW,

THE CLAIM LAW,

THE LEASE LAW;

ALSO COMPREHENSIVE CHAPTERS ON

THE HISTORY OF THE CHOCTAWS AND CHICKASAWS, THE CHICKASAW GOVERNMENT. SCHOOL SYSTEM, INTER-TRIBAL RELATIONS, GEOGRAPHY OF COUNTRY, STATUS OF FREEDMEN, NON-CITIZENS, DISFRANCHISED CITIZENS, JURISDICTION OF U. S. COURT AND THE ALLOTMENT QUESTION.

☞SENT POST-PAID TO ANY ADDRESS IN THE UNITED STATES, FOR FIFTY CENTS, BY THE CHICKASAW CHIEFTAIN PRINTING CO., ARDMORE, I. T

1891:
CHIEFTAIN PRINT,
ARDMORE. I. T.

0

Preface.

THIS PAMPHLET was compiled and written to supply the lack of authentic information among many residents of the Chickasaw Nation relative to the treaties, history, laws and affairs of the Chickasaw Indians. The statutes of the nation are in the possession of few non-citizens, hence many are ignorant of the tribal laws which affect their residence in the country. Although condensed as much as possible, the reader will find that this work covers the field quite thoroughly and is in the main reliable.

Very respectfully,

R. W. McADAM.

TREATY OF 1855.

ARTICLES OF AGREEMENT AND CONVENTION BETWEEN THE UNITED STATES AND THE CHOCTAW AND CHICKASAW TRIBES OF INDIANS MADE AND CONCLUDED AT THE CITY OF WASHINGTON, THE TWENTY-SECOND DAY OF JUNE, A. D. ONE THOUSAND EIGHT HUNDRED AND FIFTY-FIVE.

WHEREAS, The political connection heretofore existing between the Choctaw and Chickasaw tribes of Indians has given rise to unhappy and injurious dissensions and controversies among them, which render necessary a readjustment of their relations to each other and to the United States; and whereas, the United States desire that the Choctaw Indians shall relinquish all claim to any territory west of the one hundredth degree of west longitude, and, also, to make provisions for the permanent settlement within the Choctaw country of the Wichita and certain other tribes or bands of Indians, for which purpose the Choctaws and Chickasaws are willing to lease on reasonable terms to the United States, that portion of their common territory which is west of the ninety-eighth degree of west longitude, and whereas, the Choctaws contend that, by a just and fair construction of the Treaty of September 27, 1830, they are of right entitled to the net proceeds of the lands ceded by them to the United States under said Treaty, and have proposed that the question of their right to the same, together with the whole subject-matter of their unsettled claims, whether national or individual, against the United States, arising under the various provisions of said Treaty, shall be referred to the Senate of the United States for adjudication and adjustment; and whereas, it is necessary for the simplification and better understanding of the relations between the United States and the Choctaw Indians, that all their subsisting Treaty stipulations be embodied in one comprehensive instrument.

Now, therefore, The United States of America, and the Choctaws and Chickasaws, do hereby agree and stipulate as follows, viz:

ARTICLE I.

The following shall constitute and remain the boundaries of the Choctaw and Chickasaw country, viz: Beginning at a point on the Arkansas river, one hundred paces east of old Fort Smith, where the western boundary line of the State of Arkansas crosses the said river, and running thence due south to Red river; thence up Red river to the point where the meridian of one hundred degrees of west longitude crosses the same; thence north along said meridian to the main Canadian river; thence down said river to its junction with the Arkansas river; thence down said river to the place of beginning.

And pursuant to an Act of Congress approved May 28, 1830, the United States do hereby forever secure and guarantee the lands embraced within the said limits to the members of the Choctaw and Chickasaw tribes, their heirs and successors, to be held in common; so that each and every member of either tribe shall have an equal, undivided interest in the whole; Provided, however, no part thereof shall ever be sold without the consent of both tribes; and that said land shall revert to the United States if said Indians and their heirs become extinct or abandon the same.

ARTICLE II.

A district for the Chickasaws is hereby established, bounded as follows, to-wit: Beginning on the north bank of Red river, at the mouth of Island Bayou, where it empties into Red river, about twenty-six miles on a straight line, between the mouth of False Wachitta; thence running a northwesterly course along the main channel of said bayou, to the junction of three prongs of said bayou, nearest the dividing ridge between Wachitta and Low Blue rivers, as laid down on Captain R. L. Hunter's map; thence northerly along the eastern prong of Island bayou to its source; thence due north to the Canadian river; thence west along the main Canadian to the ninety-eighth degree of west longitude; thence south to Red river; and thence down Red river to the beginning; Provided, however, if the line running due north, from the eastern source of Island bayou, to the main Canadian, shall not include Allen's or Wapanucka Academy within the Chickasaw district, then an offset shall be made from said line, so as to leave said academy two miles within the Chickasaw district, north, west and south from the lines of boundary.

ARTICLE III.

The remainder of the country held in common by the Choctaws and Chickasaws shall constitute the Choctaw district, and their officers and people shall at all times have the right of safe conduct and free passage through the Chickasaw district.

ARTICLE IV.

The government and laws now in operation, and not incompatible with this instrument, shall be and remain in full force and effect within the limits of this Chickasaw district, until the Chickasaws shall adopt a constitution, and enact laws, superceding, abrogating, or changing the same. And all judicial proceedings within said district, commencing prior to the adoption of a Constitution and By-laws by the Chickasaws, shall be conducted and determined according to existing laws.

ARTICLE V.

The members of either the Choctaw or the Chickasaw tribes shall have the right, freely, to settle within the jurisdiction of the other, and shall thereupon be entitled to all the rights, privileges and immunities of citizens thereof; but no member of either tribe shall be entitled to participate in the funds belonging to the other tribe. Citizens of both tribes shall have the right to institute and prosecute suits in the courts of either, under such regulations as may from time to time be prescribed by their respective Legislatures.

ARTICLE VI.

Any person duly charged with a criminal offense against the laws of either the Choctaw or Chickasaw tribe, and escaping into the jurisdiction of the other, shall be promptly surrendered upon the demand of the proper authorities of the tribe within whose jurisdiction the offense shall be alleged to have been committed.

ARTICLE VII.

So far as may be compatible with the Constitution of the United States and the laws made in pursuance thereof, regulating trade and intercourse with the Indian tribes, the Choctaws and Chickasaws shall be secured in the unrestricted right of self-government, and full jurisdiction over persons and property within their respective limits; excepting however, all persons with their property who are not by birth adoption, or otherwise, citizens or members of either the Choctaw or Chickasaw tribe; and all persons, not being citizens or members of either tribe, found within their limits, shall be considered intruders, and be removed from and kept out of the same by the United States Agent, assisted, if necessary, by the military, with the following exceptions, viz: Such individuals as are now or may be in the employment of the Government, and their families; those peacefully traveling or temporarily sojourning in the country or trading therein under license from the proper authority of the United States, and such as may be permitted by the Choctaws or Chickasaws, with the assent of the United States Agent, to reside within their limits, without becoming citizens or members of either of said tribes.

ARTICLE VIII.

In consideration of the foregoing stipulations, and immediately upon the ratification of this convention, there shall be paid to the Choctaws, in such manner as their National Council shall direct, out of the National fund of the Chickasaws, held in trust by the United States, the sum of one hundred and fifty thousand dollars.

ARTICLE IX.

The Choctaw Indians do hereby absolutely and forever quit-claim and relinquish to the United States all their right, title and interest in and to all lands west of the one hundredth degree of west longitude, and the Choctaws and Chickasaws do hereby lease to the United States all that portion of their common territory west of the ninety-eighth degree of west longitude, for the permanent settlement of the Wichita and such other tribes or bands of Indians as the Government may desire to locate therein; excluding, however, all the Indians of New Mexico, and also those whose usual ranges at present are north of the Arkansas river, and whose permanent locations are north of the Canadian river, but including those bands whose permanent ranges are south of the Canadian or between it and the Arkansas, which Indians shall be subject to the exclusive control of the United States, under such rules and regulations, not inconsistent with the rights and interests of the Choctaws and Chickasaws, as may from time to time be prescribed by the President for their government; provided, however, the territory so leased shall remain open to settlement by Choctaws and Chickasaws as heretofore.

[NOTE. Where the asterisks [*] appear they denote omissions of sections of no importance at this time.

TREATY OF 1866.

ARTICLES OF AGREEMENT AND CONVENTION BETWEEN THE UNITED STATES AND THE CHOCTAW AND CHICKASAW NATIONS OF INDIANS MADE AND CONCLUDED AT THE CITY OF WASHINGTON, THE TWENTY-EIGHTH DAY OF APRIL, A. D. ONE THOUSAND EIGHT HUNDRED AND SIXTY-SIX.

ARTICLE I.

Permanent peace and friendship are hereby established between the United States and said Nations; and the Choctaws and Chickasaws do hereby bind themselves respectively to use their influence, and to make every exertion to induce Indians of the plains to maintain peaceful relations with each other, with other Indians, and with the United States.

ARTICLE II.

The Choctaws and Chickasaws hereby covenant and agree that henceforth neither slavery, nor involuntary servitude, otherwise than in punishment of crime, whereof the parties shall have been duly convicted in accordance with the laws applicable to all members of the particular Nation, shall ever exist in said Nations.

ARTICLE III.

The Choctaws and Chickasaws, in consideration of the sum of $300,000, hereby cede to the United States the territory west of the 98th degree, west longitude, known as the leased district, provided that the said sum shall be invested and held by the United States at an interest not less than five per cent., in trust for the said Nations, until the Legislatures of the Choctaw and Chickasaw Nations respectively shall have made such laws, rules and regulations as may be necessary to give all persons of African descent, resident in the said Nations at the date of the Treaty of Fort Smith, and their descendants, heretofore held in slavery among said Nations, all the rights, privileges and Immunities, including the right of suffrage, of citizens of said Nations, except in the annuities, monies, and public domain claimed by or belonging to said Nations respectively; and also to give to such persons who were residents as aforesaid, and their descendants, forty acres each of the land of said Nations on the same terms as the Choctaws and Chickasaws, to be selected on the survey of said land, after the Choctaws and Chickasaws and Kansas Indians have made their selections as herein provided; and immediately on the enactment of such laws, rules and regulations, the said sum of $300,000 shall be paid to the said Choctaw and Chickasaw Nations in the proportion of three-fourths to the former and one-fourth to the latter, less such sum, at the rate of one hundred dollars per capita, as shall be sufficient to pay such persons of African descent before referred to as, within ninety days after the passage of such laws, rules and regulations, shall elect to remove and actually remove from the said Nations respectively. And should the said laws, rules and regulations not be made by the Legislatures of the said Nations respectively, within two years from the ratification of this Treaty, then the said sum of three hundred thousand dollars shall cease to be held in trust for the said Choctaw and Chickasaw Nations, and be held for the use and benefit of such of said persons of African descent as the United States shall remove from the said territory in such manner as the United States shall deem proper, the United States agreeing, within ninety days from the expiration of the said two years, to remove from said Nations all such persons of African descent as may be willing to remove; those remaining or returning after having been removed from said Nations to have no benefit of said sum of three hundred thousand dollars, or any part thereof, but shall be upon the same footing as other citizens of the United States in the said Nations.

ARTICLE IV.

The said Nations further agree that all negroes, not otherwise disqualified or disabled, shall be competent witnesses in all civil and criminal suits and proceedings in the Choctaw and Chickasaw Courts, any law to the contrary notwithstanding, and they fully recognize the right of the freedmen to a fair remuneration on reasonable and equitable contracts for their labor, which the law should aid them to enforce. And they agree, on the part of their respective Nations, that all laws shall be equal in their operation upon Choctaws, Chickasaws and negroes, and that no distinction affecting the latter shall at any time be made, and that they shall be treated with kindness and be protected against injury; and they further agree, that while the said freedmen, now in the Choctaw and Chickasaw Nations, remain in said Nations respectively, they shall be entitled to as much land as they may cultivate for the support of themselves and families in cases where they do not support themselves by hiring, not interfering with existing improvements without the consent of the occupant, it being understood that in the event of the making of the laws, rules and regulations aforesaid, the forty acres aforesaid shall stand in place of the land cultivated as last aforesaid.

* * * * * *

ARTICLE VI.

The Choctaws and Chickasaws hereby grant a right of way through their lands to any company or companies which shall be duly authorized by Congress or by the Legislatures of said Nations, respectively, and which shall, with the express consent and approbation of the Secretary of the Interior, undertake to construct a railroad through the Choctaw and Chickasaw Nations from the north to the south thereof, and from the east to the west side thereof, in accordance with the provisions of the 18th Article of the Treaty of June 22, 1855, which provides that for any property taken or destroyed in the construction thereof. full compensation shall be made to the party or parties injured, to be ascertained and determined in such manner as the President of the United States shall direct. But such railroad company or companies, with its or their agents and employes, shall be subject to the laws of the United States relating to intercourse with Indian tribes, and also to such rules and regulations as may be prescribed by the Secretary of the Interior for that purpose. And it is also stipulated and agreed that the Nation through which the road or roads aforesaid shall pass may subscribe to the stock of the particular company or companies such amount or amounts as they may be able to pay for in alternate sections of unoccupied lands for a space of six miles on each side of said road or roads, at a price per acre to be agreed upon between said Choctaw and Chickasaw Nations and the said company or companies, subject to the approval of the President of the United States; Provided, however, that said land, thus subscribed shall not be sold, or demised, or occupied by any one not a citizen of the Choctaw or Chickasaw Nations, according to their laws and recognized usages; Provided, that the officers, servants and employes of such companies necessary to the construction and management of said road or roads shall not be excluded from such company as their respective functions may require, they being subject to the Indian intercourse law, and such rules and regulations as may be established by the Secretary of the Interior; And provided also, that the stock thus subscribed by either of said Nations shall have the force and effect of first mortgage bond on all that part of said road, appurtenances and equipments situated and used within said Nations respectively, and shall be a perpetual lien on the same, and the said Nations shall have the right from year to year, to elect or receive their equitable proportion of declared dividends or profits on their said stock, or interest on the par value at the rate of six per cent. per annum.

2. And it is further declared, in this connection, that as fast as sections of twenty miles in length are completed, with the rails and ready for use, with all water and other stations necessary to the use thereof, as a first-class road, the said company or companies shall become entitled to patents for the alternate sections aforesaid, and may proceed to dispose thereof in the manner herein provided for, subject to the approval of the Secretary of the Interior.

3. And it is further declared, also, in case of one or more of said alternate sections being occupied by any member or members of said Nations respectively, so that the same cannot be transferred to the said company or companies, that the said Nation or Nations, respectively, may select any unoccupied section or sections, as near as circumstances will permit, to the said width of six miles on each side of said road or roads, and convey the same as an equivalent for the section or sections so occupied as aforesaid.

ARTICLE VII.

The Choctaws and Chickasaws agree to such legislation as Congress and the President of the United States may deem necessary for the better administration of justice and the protection of the rights of person and property within the Indian Territory; Provided, however, such legislation shall not in anywise interfere with or annul their present tribal organization or their respective legislatures or judiciaries, or the rights, laws, privileges or customs of the Choctaw and Chickasaw Nations respectively.

ARTICLE VIII.

The Choctaws and Chickasaws also agree that a Council, consisting of delegates selected by each Nation or Tribe lawfully resident within the Indian Territory, to be organized as follows:

1. After the ratification of this Treaty, and as soon as may be practicable by the Secretary of the Interior, and prior to the first ses-

sion of said Assembly, a census of each tribe, lawfully resident in said Territory, shall be taken, under the direction of the Superintendent of Indian Affairs, by competent persons, to be appointed by him, whose compensation shall be fixed by the Secretary of the Interior, and paid by the United States.

2. The Council shall consist of one member from each Tribe or Nation whose population shall exceed five hundred, and an additional member for each one thousand Indians, native or adopted, or each fraction of a thousand greater than five hundred, being members of any tribe lawfully resident in said Territory, and shall be selected by the Tribes or Nations respectively who may assent to the establishment of said General Assembly; and if none should be thus formally selected by any Nation or Tribe, it shall be represented in said General Assembly by the Chief or Chiefs and head men of said Tribes, to be taken in the order of their rank as recognized in tribal usage in the number and proportions above indicated.

3. After the said census shall have been taken and completed, the Superintendent of Indian Affairs shall publish and declare to each tribe the number of members of said Council to which they shall be entitled under the provisions of this Article: and the persons so to represent the said tribes shall meet at such time and place as he shall designate, but thereafter the time and place of the sessions of the General Assembly shall be determined by itself: Provided that no session in any one year shall exceed the term of thirty days; and, provided, that the special sessions may be called whenever, in the judgment of the Secretary of the Interior, the Interests of the said tribes shall require it.

4. The General Assembly shall have power to legislate upon all subjects and matters pertaining to the intercourse and relations of the Indian tribes and Nations resident in the said territory, the arrest and extradition of criminals escaping from one tribe to another, the administration of justice between members of the several tribes of said territory, and persons other than Indians and members of said tribes or Nations, the construction of works of internal improvement, and the common defense and safety of the Nations of the said territory. All laws enacted by said Council shall take effect at the times therein provided unless suspended by the Secretary of the Interior or the President of the United States. No law shall be enacted inconsistent with the Constitution of the United States or the laws of Congress or existing Treaty stipulations with the United States: nor shall said Council legislate upon matters pertaining to the legislative, judicial or other organization laws or customs of the several tribes or Nations, except herein provided for.

5. Said Council shall be presided over by the Superintendent of Indian Affairs, or in case of his absence from any cause, the duties of the Superintendent enumerated in this Article shall be performed by such person as the Secretary of the Interior shall indicate.

6. The Secretary of the Interior shall appoint a Secretary of said Council, whose duty it shall be to keep an accurate record of the proceedings of said Council and to transmit a true copy thereof duly certified by the Superintendent of Indian Affairs, to the Secretary of

the Interior, immediately after the sessions of said Council shall terminate. He shall be paid five hundred dollars, as an annual salary, by the United States.

7. The members of said Council shall be paid by the United States four dollars per diem while in actual attendance thereon, and four dollars mileage for every twenty miles going and returning therefrom by the most direct route, to be certified by the Secretary of said Council and the presiding officer.

8. The Choctaws and Chickasaws also agree that a court or courts may be established in said territory with such jurisdiction and organization as Congress may prescribe; Provided that the same shall not interfere with the local judiciary of either of said Nations.

9. Whenever Congress shall authorize the appointment of a delegate from said territory it shall be the province of said Council to elect one from among the Nations represented in said Council.

10. And it is further agreed that the Superintendent of Indian Affairs shall be the executive of the said territory, with the title of Governor of said territory of Oklahoma, and that there shall be a Secretary of the said territory to be appointed by the said Superintendent; that the duty of said Governor, in addition to those already imposed on the Superintendent of Indian Affairs, shall be such as properly belong to an executive officer charged with the execution of the laws, which the said Council is authorized to enact under the provisions of this Treaty; and that for this purpose he shall have authority to appoint Marshal of said territory and an Interpreter; the said Marshal to appoint such deputies, to be paid by fees, as may be required to aid him in the execution of his proper functions, and be the Marshal of the principal court of said territory that may be established under the provisions of this Treaty.

11. And the said Marshal and the said Secretary shall each be entitled to a salary of $500 per annum, to be paid by the United States, and such fees in addition thereto, as shall be established by said Governor, with the approbation of the Secretary of the Interior; it being understood that the said fee lists may at any time be corrected and altered by the Secretary of the Interior, as the experience of the system proposed herein to be established shall show to be necessary, and shall in no case exceed the fees paid to Marshals of the United States for similar services. The salary of the Interpreter shall be $500, to be paid in like manner by the United States.

12. And the United States agree that in the appointment of Marshals and Deputies, preference, qualifications being equal, shall be given to competent members of said Nations, the object being to create a laudable ambition to acquire the experience necessary for political offices of importance in the respective Nations.

AND WHEREAS, It is desired by the said Choctaw and Chickasaw Nations, that the said Council should consist of an upper and lower house, it is hereby agreed that whenever a majority of the Tribes or Nations represented in said council shall desire the same, or the Congress of the United States shall so prescribe, there shall be, in addition to the Council now provided for, and which shall then constitute the lower house, and the upper house, consisting of one member from each tribe entitled to representation in the Council now provided for——the relations of the two houses to each other being such as prevail in the States of the United States; each house being authorized to choose its presiding officer and clerk to perform the duties appropriate to such offices; and it being the duty, in addition, of the clerks of each house to make out and transmit to the Territorial Secretary, fair copies of the proceedings of the respective houses immediately after their respective sessions, which copies shall be dealt with by the said Secretary as is now provided in the case of copies of the proceedings of the Council mentioned in this Act, and the said clerks shall each be entitled to the same per diem as members of the respective houses, and the presiding officers to double that sum.

* * * * * *

ARTICLE XI.

WHEREAS, The land occupied by the Choctaw and Chickasaw Nations, and described in the Treaty between the United States and said Nations of June 22, 1855, is now held by the members of said Nations in common, under the provisions of said Treaty; and whereas, it is believed that the holding of said land in severalty, will promote the general civilization of said Nations, and tend to advance their permanent welfare and the best interests of their individual members, it is hereby agreed that, should the Choctaw and Chickasaw people, through their respective Legislative Councils, agree to the survey and dividing their land on the system of the United States, the land aforesaid east of the ninety-eighth degree of west longitude shall be, in view of the arrangements hereinafter mentioned, surveyed and laid off in ranges townships, sections and parts of sections; and that for the purpose of facilitating such surveys and for the settlement and distribution of said land as hereinafter provided, there shall be established at Boggy Depot, in the Choctaw Territory, a land office; and that in making the said surveys and conducting the business of the said office, including the appointment of all necessary agents and surveyors, the same system shall be pursued which has heretofore governed in respect to the public lands of the United States, it being understood that the said surveys shall be made at the cost of the United States and by their agents and surveyors, as in the case of their own public lands, and that the officers and employes shall receive the same compensation as is paid to the officers and employes in the land offices of the United States in Kansas.

ARTICLE XII.

The maps of said surveys shall exhibit, as far as practicable, the outlines of the actual occupancy of members of the said Nations, respectively; and when they are completed, shall be returned to the said land office at Boggy Depot for inspection by all parties interested, when notice for ninety days shall be given of such return, in such manner as the legislative authorities of the said Nations, respectively shall prescribe, or in the event of the said authorities failing to give such notice in a reasonable time, in such manner as the Register of said land office shall prescribe, calling upon all parties interested to examine said maps, to the end that errors. if any, in the location of such occupancies may be corrected.

ARTICLE XIII.

The notice required in the above Article shall be given, not only in the Choctaw and Chickasaw Nations, but by publication in newspapers printed in the States of Mississippi and Tennessee, Louisiana, Texas, Arkansas and Alabama, to the end that such Choctaws and Chickasaws as yet remain outside of the Choctaw and Chickasaw Nations, may be informed and have oppportunity to exercise the rights hereby given to resident Choctaws and Chickasaws; provided, that before any such absent Choctaw or Chickasaw shall be permitted to select for him or herself, or others, as hereinafter provided, he or she shall satisfy the Register of the Land office of his or her intention, or the intention of the party for whom the selection is to be made, to become bona fide residents in the said Nation within five years from the time of selection; and should the said absentee fail to remove into said Nation, and occupy and commence an improvement on the land selected within the time aforesaid, the said selection shall be cancelled, and the land thereafter shall be discharged from all claim on account thereof.

ARTICLE XIV.

At the expiration of the ninety days aforesaid, the legislative authorities of the said Nations, respectively, shall have the right to select one-quarter section of land in each of the counties of said Nations, respectively, in trust for the establishment of seats of justice therein, and also as many quarter sections as the said Legislative Councils may deem proper for the permanent endowment of schools, seminaries and colleges in said Nation, provided such selection shall not embrace or interfere with any improvement in the actual occupation of any member of the particular Nation without his consent; and provided the proceeds of sale of the quarter sections selected for seats of justice shall be appropriated for the erection or improvement of public buildings in the county in which it is located.

ARTICLE XV.

At the expiration of the ninety days' notice aforesaid, the selection which is to change the tenure of the land in the Choctaw and Chickasaw Nations from a holding in common to a holding in severalty shall take place, when every Choctaw and Chickasaw shall have the right to one-quarter section of land, whether male or female, adult or minor, and if in actual possession or occupancy of land improved or cultivated by him or her, shall have a prior right to the quarter section in which his or her improvement lies; and every infant shall have selected for him or her a quarter section of land in such location as the father of such infant, if there be a father living, and if no father living, then the mother, or guardian, and should there be neither father, mother nor guardian, then as the Probate Judge of the county, acting for the best interests of such infant, shall select.

ARTICLE XVI.

Should an actual occupant of land desire. at any time prior to the commencement of the surveys aforesaid, to abandon his improvement, and select and improve other land, so as to obtain the prior right of selection thereof, he or she shall be at liberty to do so; in which event the improvement so abandoned shall be open to selection by other parties; Provided, that nothing herein contained shall authorize the nullification of improvements so as to increase the quantity of land beyond what a party would be entitled to at the date of this Treaty.

ARTICLE XVII.

No selection to be made under this Treaty shall be permitted to deprive or interfere with the continued occupation by the missionaries established in the respective Nations, of their several missionary establishments; it being the wish of the parties hereto to promote and foster an influence, so largely conducive to civilization and refinement. Should any missionary who has been engaged in missionary labor for five consecutive years before the date of this Treaty in the said Nations, or either of them, or three consecutive years prior to the late rebellion, and who, if absent from the said Nations, may desire to return, wish to select a quarter section of land, with a view to a permanent home for himself and family, he shall have the privilege of doing so, provided no selection shall include any public buildings, schools or seminary; and a quantity of land not exceeding six hundred and forty acres, to be selected according to legal subdivisions, in one body, and to include their improvements, is hereby granted to every religious society or denomination which has erected, or which, with the consent of the Indians, may hereafter erect buildings within the Choctaw and Chickasaw country for missionary or educational purposes; but no land thus granted, nor the buildings which have been or may be erected thereon, shall ever be sold or otherwise disposed of, except with the consent of the Legislatures of said Nations respectively, and approval of the Secretary of the Interior; and whenever such lands or buildings shall be sold or disposed of, the proceeds thereof shall be applied, under the direction of the Secretary of the Interior, to the support and maintainance of other similar establishments for the benefit of the Choctaws and Chickasaws, and such other persons as may hereafter become members of their Nations, according to their laws, customs and usages.

ARTICLE XVIII.

In making a selection for children, the parent shall have a prior right to select land adjacent to his own improvements or selection, provided such selection shall be made within thirty days from the time at which selections under this Treaty commence.

ARTICLE XIX

The manner of selecting as aforesaid shall be by an entry with the Register of the land office, and all selections shall be made to conform to the legal subdivisions of the said lands, as shown by the surveys aforesaid on the maps aforesaid, it being understood that nothing herein contained is to be construed to confine a party selecting to one section, but he may take contiguous parts of sections by legal subdivisions in different sections, not exceeding together a quarter section.

ARTICLE XX.

Prior to any entries being made under the foregoing provisions, proof of improvements, or actual cultivation, as well as the number of persons for whom a parent or guardian, or Probate Judge of the county proposes to select, and of their right to select, and of his or her authority to select for them, shall be made to the Register and Receiver of the land office, under regulations to be prescribed by the Secretary of the Interior.

ARTICLE XXI.

In every township the sections of land numbered 16 and 36 shall be reserved for the support of schools in said township; Provided, that if the same has been already occupied by a party or parties having the right to select it, or it shall be so sterile as to be unavailable, the legislative authorities of the particular Nations shall have the right to select such other unoccupied sections as they may think proper.

ARTICLE XXII.

The right of selection hereby given shall not authorize the selection of any land required by the United States as a military post, or Indian agency, not exceeding one mile square, which, when abandoned, shall revert to the Nation in which the land lies.

ARTICLE XXIII.

The Register of the land office shall inscribe in a suitable book or books, in alphabetical order, the name of every individual for whom a selection shall be made, his or her age and a description of the land selected.

ARTICLE XXIV.

WHEREAS, it may be difficult to give each occupant of an improvement a quarter section of land, or even a smaller subdivision which shall include such improvement, in consequence of such improvements lying in towns, villages or hamlets, the legislative authorities of the respective Nations shall have power where, in their discretion, they think it expedient, to lay off in town lots any section or part of a section so occupied, to which lots the actual occupants, being citizens of the respective Nations, shall have pre-emptive right, and upon paying into the Treasury of the particular Nation the price of the land as fixed by the respective Legislatures, exclusive of the value of said improvement, shall receive a conveyance thereof. Such occupant shall not be prejudiced thereby in his right to his selection elsewhere. The town-lots which may be unoccupied shall be disposed of, for the benefit of the particular Nation, as the legislative authorities may direct from time to time. When the number of occupants of the same quarter section shall not be such as to authorize the legislative authorities to lay out the same, or any part thereof, into town lots, they may make such regulations for the disposition thereof, as they may deem proper, either by subdivision of the same, so as to accommodate the actual occupants, or by giving the right of prior choice to the first occupant in point of time, upon paying the others for their improvements, to be valued in such way as the legislative authorities shall prescribe, or otherwise. All occupants retaining their lots under this section, and desiring, in addition, to make a selection, must pay for the lots so retained, as in the case of town lots. And any Choctaw or Chickasaw who may desire to select a sectional division, other than that on which his homestead is, without abandoning the latter, shall have the right to purchase the homestead sectional division at such price as the respective Legislatures may prescribe.

ARTICLE XXV.

During ninety days from the expiration of ninety days' notice aforesaid, the Choctaws and Chickasaws shall have the exclusive right to make selections, as aforesaid, and at the end of that time the several parties shall be entitled to patents for their respective selections to be issued by the President of the United States, and countersigned by the chief executive of the Nation in which the land lies, and recorded in the records of the executive office of the particular Nations, and copies of the said patents, under seal shall be evidence in any court of law or equity.

ARTICLE XXVI.

The right here given to Choctaws and Chickasaws respectively, shall extend to all persons who have become citizens by adoption or intermarriage of either of said Nations, or who may hereafter become such.

ARTICLE XXVII.

In the event of disputes arising in regard to the rights of parties to select particular quarter sections or other divisions of said land, or in regard to the adjustment of boundaries, so as to make them conform to the legal divisions and subdivisions, such disputes shall be settled by the Register of the land office and the chief executive officer of the Nation in which the land lies in a summary way, after hearing the parties; and if said Register and chief officer cannot agree, the two to call in a third party, who shall constitute a third referee, the decision of any two of whom shall be final, without appeal.

ARTICLE XXVIII.

Nothing contained in any law of either of the said Nations shall prevent parties entitled to make selections contiguous to each other; and the Choctaw and Chickasaw Nations hereby agree to repeal all laws inconsistent with this provision.

ARTICLE XXIX.

Selections made under this Treaty shall, to the extent of one quarter section, including the homestead or dwelling, be inalienable for the period of twenty-one years from the date of such selection, and upon the death of the party in possession shall descend according to the laws of the Nation where the land lies; and in the event of his or her death without heirs, the said quarter section shall escheat to and become the property of the Nation.

* * * * * * *

ARTICLE XXXII.

At the expiration of two years, or sooner, if the President of the United States shall so direct, from the completion of the surveys and maps aforesaid, the officers of the land offices aforesaid shall deliver to the executive departments of the Choctaw and Chickasaw Nations, respectively, all such documents as may be necessary to elucidate the the land title as settled according to this Treaty, and forward copies thereof, with the field notes, records and other papers pertaining to said titles, to the Commissioner of the General Land Office; and thereafter grants of lands and patents therefor shall be issued in such manner as the legislative authorities of said Nations may provide for all the unselected portions of the Choctaw and Chickasaw districts as defined by the Treaty of June 22, 1855.

ARTICLE XXXIII.

All lands selected as herein provided shall thereafter be held in severalty of the respective parties and the unselected land shall be the common property of the Choctaw and Chickasaw Nations in their corporate capacities, subject to the joint control of their legislative authorities.

ARTICLE XXXIV.

Should any Choctaw or Chickasaw be prevented from selecting for him or herself during the ninety days aforesaid, the failure to do so shall not authorize another to select the quarter section containing his improvement, but he may at any time make his selection thereof, subject to having his boundaries made to conform to legal divisions as aforesaid.

ARTICLE XXXV.

Should the selections aforesaid not be made before the transfer of the land records to the executive authorities of said Nations, respectively, they shall be made according to such regulations as the legislative authorities of the two Nations, respectively, may prescribe, to the end that full justice and equity may be done to the citizens of the respective territories.

ARTICLE XXXVI.

Should any land that has been selected under the provisions of this Treaty be abandoned and left uncultivated for the space of seven years by the party selecting the same, or his heirs except in the case of infants under the age of twenty-one years, or married women, or persons non compos mentis, the legislative authorities of the Nation where such land lies, may either rent the same for the benefit of those interested, or dispose of the same otherwise for their benefit, and may pass all laws necessary to give effect to this provision.

* * * * * * *

ARTICLE XXXVIII.

Every white person who, having married a Choctaw or Chickasaw, resides in the said Choctaw or Chickasaw Nations, or who has been adopted by the legislative authorities, is to be deemed a member of said Nation, and shall be subject to the laws of the Choctaw and Chickasaw Nations according to his domicile, and to prosecution and trial before their tribunals, and to punishment according to their laws in all respects, as though he was a native Choctaw or Chickasaw.

ARTICLE XXXIX.

No person shall expose goods or other articles for sale as a trader, without a permit; but no license shall be required to authorize any member of the Choctaw or Chickasaw Nations to trade in the Choctaw or Chickasaw country, who is authorized by the proper authority of the Nation, nor to authorize Choctaws or Chickasaws to sell flour, meal, meat, fruit and other provisions, stock, wagons, agricultural implements, or tools brought from the United States into said country.

* * * * * * *

ARTICLE XLI.

All persons who are members of the Choctaw or Chickasaw Nations, and are not otherwise disqualified or disabled, shall hereafter be competent witnesses in all civil and criminal suits and proceedings in any courts of the United States, any law to the contrary notwithstanding.

ARTICLE XLII.

The Choctaw and Chickasaw Nations shall deliver up persons accused of crime against the United States, who may be found within their respective limits, on the requisition of the Governor of any State, for a crime committed against the laws of said State, and upon the requisition of the judge of the District Court of the United States, for the district within which the crime was committed.

ARTICLE XLIII.

The United States promise and agree that no white person, except officers, agents and employes of the Government and of any internal improvement company, or persons traveling through or temporarily sojourning in the said Nations or either of them, shall be permitted to go into said territory, unless formally incorporated and naturalized by the joint action of the authorities of both Nations into one of the said Nations of Choctaws and Chickasaws, according to their laws, customs or usages, but this Article is not to be construed to affect parties heretofore adopted, or to prevent the employment temporarily of white persons who are teachers, mechanics or skilled in agriculture, or to prevent the legislative authorities of the respective Nations from authorizing such works of internal improvement as they may deem essential to the welfare and prosperity of the community, or to be taken to interfere with or invalidate any action which has heretofore been had in this connection by either of the said Nations.

ARTICLE XLIV.

Postoffices shall be established and maintained by the United States at convenient places in the Choctaw and Chickasaw Nations, to and from which the mails shall be carried at reasonable intervals, at the rates of postage prevailing in the United States.

ARTICLE XLV.

All the rights, privileges and immunities heretofore possessed by said Nations or individuals thereof, or to which they were entitled under the Treaties and legislation heretofore made and had in connection with them, shall be, and are hereby declared to be, in full force, so far as they are consistent with the provisions of this Treaty.

ARTICLE XLVI.

Of the monies stipulated to be paid to the Choctaws and Chickasaws under this Treaty for the cession of the leased district, and the admission of the Kansas Indians among them, the sum of $150,000 shall be advanced and paid to the Choctaws, and $50,000 to the Chickasaws, through their respective Treasurers, as soon as practicable after the

CHOCTAWS AND CHICKASAWS.

TRADITIONS, EARLY HISTORY AND PROGRESS.

IF credence is to be given tradition, the Choctaws, Chickasaws, Muskogees (Creeks) and Seminoles were many centuries ago one tribe, occupying the entire southeastern portion of the United States, from the Mississippi to the Savannah river. Internecine rebellions, engendered by factional quarrels and the jealousies of ambitious chiefs, ultimately divided the great nation into four tribes, which, in the course of time, learned different dialects, customs and laws. The Seminoles claimed as their domain the peninsula country, now Florida; the Creeks the region north of the Seminoles, comprising a part of eastern Alabama, Georgia, and perhaps part of South Carolina; the Choctaws a large portion of Alabama and the southern half of Mississippi; the Chickasaws, the lands to the north of the Choctaws, comprising northern Mississippi and a portion of west Tennessee. When DeSota explored this region (1540), these tribes occupied the territory in the manner described.

The Choctaws and Chickasaws had their traditions, many of which have been preserved to this day. In the old Choctaw country is a cave in a hill which the Choctaws held as sacred, claiming that the first parents of their people came from this cave by magic. The Chickasaws have another tradition. Long centuries ago, when the Choctaws and Chickasaws were one people, they dwelt far to the west of the Mississippi. Driven by the ferocious northern Indians from their country, they journeyed toward the sunrise many moons, under the guardianship of a sacred dog, led onward by a magic pole, which they planted in the ground every night, and in the morning traveled toward the direction the pole leaned. At last, after crossing vast deserts, boundless forests and dismal swamps, leaving thousands of their dead along the way, they reached the great Father of Waters. While crossing the Mississippi, the sacred dog was drowned. Following the direction indicated by the magic pole, they continued eastward to the banks of the Alabama river, where the pole, after being unsettled for several days, pointed distinctly southwest. They proceeded in that direction to the southern portion of Mississippi, where the pole planted itself firmly in a perpendicular line. This was the omen for permanent settlement, and here the tribe dwelt. Tradition concerning the rebellion and formation of an independent tribe by the Chickasaws, is very vague. The word Chikasha (Chickasaw), in the Choctaw tongue, signifies rebel, the latter tribe giving its rebellious offshoot that name, which the Chickasaws evidently accepted as their distinctive tribal name.

It might be interesting here to dwell briefly upon the primitive life of these southern tribes. It is a mistake to class the North American Indians as one family of savages. As well confound the aboriginal inhabitants of Europe. When the early navigators touched upon the unknown shores of the Gulf of Mexico, the red men who greeted them were not savages, living exclusively by the chase and the spoils of war. In a measure, these Indians were civilized. They had their rude arts, laws, customs and religion, inferior but somewhat similar to those of the Aztecs and Incas, which leads to the belief that the magic pole tradition had its origin in an exodus of these tribes from Mexico. The theory that the Chickasaws and Choctaws were an offshot of the civilized Aztecs, has some foundation. They were not primarily a warlike race. Their disposition was not ferocious, although they were capable of waging long and bloody wars when driven to such an extremity by perfidy and wrong. The ancient government of the Choctaws and Chickasaws was democratic and simple. Their ruler was called King, but his authority was abridged by the powers of the council, which was made and unmade at will by the people. Their ideas of justice were based on principles of equity. Virtue, truth and honesty were, it is said, a striking characteristic. Their methods of agriculture were crude, but it is certain that they cultivated the great Indian cereal and prepared it for food by crushing, the meal being baked as bread, or the grain parched or boiled whole. Their theology was beautifully poetic and largely a worship of the heart, without the elaborate and barbarous rites of the sun-worshippers further south. To their simple imagining the manifestations of the Great Spirit were constantly heard and seen in the works of nature. Their daily life was one of devotion to quaint and pretty superstitions and spirit-worship. When De Soto, De Luna, and other white explorers first penetrated their country, they found a race hospitable, virtuous, peaceable and happy. They were met as gods, and lavished with gifts and kindness. They requited this generous treatment by treachery, rapine and conquest.

After the white man had come among these Indians with the innovations which we proudly term civilization, the history of the Choctaws and Chickasaws is the history of the subjugation of the red race. Contact with the white man's civilization began the work of extermination and implanted in hitherto trustful breasts the seeds of hatred and revenge. The Chickasaws and Choctaws were fearfully decimated by wars with the Europeans and other tribes. During the early explorations it is said they had 15,000 warriors, while in 1720 the two tribes could muster less than 1,000 fighting men. The Choctaws allied themselves to the French in the war against the Natchez, whom the Chickasaws aided. The two latter tribes were badly beaten. From 1540 to the establishment of the American republic, the Chickasaws and Choctaws were almost constantly at war. As progress followed the star of empire westward, the rights of these Indians, as they understood them, were more and more circumscribed. In 1765 the Chickasaws made their first general treaty with General Oglethorpe, of Georgia, and in 1786, after the colonies had gained their independence, both the Chickasaws and Choctaws made a treaty at Hopewell and were guaranteed peaceable possession of their lands. From the date of this treaty the Choctaws and Chickasaws have kept faith with the federal government. The Chickasaws, in the treaty of 1834, boast "that they have ever been faithful and friendly to the people of this country; that they have never raised the tomahawk to shed the blood of an American."

As early as 1800 the encroachments of the whites filled these people with a desire to emigrate beyond the Mississippi, and many families did so. In 1803 it was estimated that 500 families had departed, mostly Choctaws. The whole nation would have gone but for the opposition of the Spaniards and the western tribes. In the war of 1812 and the Creek war, the Choctaws and Chickasaws did valiant service for the United States. In 1820 the Choctaws ceded to the government a part of their territory for lands west of Arkansas. The establishment of state governments over their country, to whose laws they were subject, still further dissatisfied the Choctaws and Chickasaws, who, as their treaty put it, "being ignorant of the language and laws of the white man, cannot understand nor obey them." The Choctaws were the first to emigrate. By the treaty of Dancing Rabbit creek, in 1830, they ceded the remainder of their lands, 19,000,000 acres in all, and received 20,000,000 acres in the country west of Arkansas, with $2,225,-000 in money and goods. After the ratification of this treaty, nearly the entire Choctaw tribe emigrated to the new lands. Those who chose to remain behind were given allotments by the government, and the residue lands were sold to white settlers. In 1805, 1816 and 1818, the Chickasaws ceded all their lands north of Mississippi, on liberal terms. Many of the tribe joined the Choctaw exodus to the west. In 1822 there were 3,625 Chickasaws remaining in Mississippi. In 1832 the Chickasaw Nation began negotiations with the United States for the sale of their reservation, consisting of 6,442,400 acres, and the treaty was ratified the following year. The conditions of the sale were that the government should sell the land to the highest bidder, the Chickasaws to receive the sum so derived, after the expense of the survey and sale had been deducted. It was the purpose of the Chickasaws to seek a new home in the west, whither their neighbors, the Choctaws, had gone; but in case a desirable location could not be procured, or certain members of the tribe should prefer to remain behind, the Chickasaws were allowed to take allotments pending their emigration. The government agreed to furnish funds sufficient to defray the expenses of the journey, and for one year's provisions after their arrival at their new home, the amount thus appropriated to be refunded from the receipts of the sale. The amount received by the Chickasaws from the sale of these lands was $3,646,000. The Chickasaws determined to create a perpetual fund from the sale of their lands, the money to be invested by the United States, the interest derived therefrom to be used for national purposes. In 1834 the final treaty in reference to the cession of the Chickasaw lands and the removal of the tribe, was made at Washington.

The commissioners sent by the Chickasaw Nation to seek out a new home in the west, entered successfully into negotiations with the Choctaws for an interest in their lately acquired lands beyond the

Mississippi. In 1837 a treaty between the two tribes was ratified near Fort Towson, in the Choctaw Nation, by which the Chickasaws, for the consideration of $530,000, were ceded a district in the Choctaw country west of the Choctaw Nation proper. The conditions of this sale were that the Chickasaws should participate jointly with the Choctaws in the tribal government, with equal rights and privileges, the land to be held in common by both, neither tribe having a right to dispose of its interest without the consent of the other. Each tribe reserved to itself the right to control and manage its own funds, invested in Washington. The lands set apart for the Chickasaws were known as the Chickasaw District of the Choctaw Nation, and members of either tribe were given the privilege of locating in either the Choctaw or Chickasaw countries proper.

During the emigration of the Chickasaws to their new home, smallpox broke out, carrying off nearly 700 of the movers. They did not all settle in the Chickasaw District, but many scattered through the Choctaw country.

As a body, the Chickasaws did not advance as rapidly as the Choctaws, their large annuities encouraging idleness and improvidence. Their efforts at agriculture were insignificant, such work as there was being performed by slaves. Their first school was not established until 1851. The political relations between the two tribes, under the provisions of the treaty of 1837, were far from amicable, as, instead of equal represeutation as they expected, they were allowed only in proportion to population and were therefore a powerless minority, the Choctaws outnumbering and hence outvoting the Chickasaws, thereby controling the national offices and affairs of government. The Chickasaws, feeling themselves agrieved, appealed to the President of the United States, and on paying $150,000 to the Choctaws, obtained, by treaty of 1855, a political separation from the Choctaws, and a complete title to the Chickasaw District. The Chickasaws then established their own government, and though closely allied by treaty and other relations to the Choctaws, have maintained an independent government and distinct geographical boundaries.

By a liberal policy extended toward intermarried whites and stock-raisers within their boundaries, and through their efforts in the direction of education, the progress of the Chickasaws and Choctaws was gradual until the great civil war. The agents of these nations took sides with the seceding states, and the sympathies of the Indians were naturally with the Confederate States. The Choctaws and Chickasaws furnished several thousand men for the cause and negotiated treaties with the Confederate government. The nations suffered considerably by the war, losing nearly one-fourth of their population, much stock, and of course their slaves. The United States held that by the part taken by the tribal government in the war, they had forfeited all their rights, which were, however, restored under certain conditions, and the treaty of 1866 was made. This treaty, the provisions of which supersede all conflicting provisions of former treaties, is the basis of all laws pertaining to the intercourse of the Choctaws and Chickasaws with the federal government. The allotment and governmental provisions of the treaty of 1866 have never been complied with, and vexed questions have resulted therefrom.

The progress of the Choctaws and Chickasaws since the war has been remarkable, although the latter, perhaps, have outstripped the former. A lapse of a quarter of a century has wrought great changes in the condition of these Indians. Amalgamation and association with the Anglo-Saxon have in a great measure accomplished the ends of civilization. As a people the Choctaws and Chickasaws are well-to-do, being the possessors of a vast area of of the most fertile lands in the southwest, rich in timber, mineral and other natural resources. They are peculiarly a nation of landlords, their tenants comprising over nine-tenths of the population of the two nations. According to the census of 1890, the Choctaws number 9,996 and the Chickasaws 3,464. In the Chickasaw Nation alone there 49,444 non-citizen whites, and about 3,000 negroes. The educational system of the two nations, so far as the funds at their command for this purpose are concerned, should be surpassed by that of no people on earth, and indeed it is excellent. The Chickasaws have $1,308,695 as an invested fund with the United States, which pays them an annual interest of $78,409. The Choctaws have $549,549, with an annual interest of $32,344. In addition to the revenue derived from the sale of their Mississippi lands, these governments obtain a handsome revenue by licensed traders' and permit taxes, mining royalties, &c., paid by non-citizens—individuals and corporations—besides the revenues arising from the operation of their several courts. The total annual revenue thus derived is in the neighborhood of $130,000.

Few events historically interesting have transpired in Choctaw and Chickasaw affairs since the re-establishment of their respective governments. Several years ago, the Choctaws, in accordance with the treaty of '66, adopted their freedmen, contrary to the wishes of their Chickasaw neighbors, but refused to accept the allotment of their lands in severalty. The Chickasaws acted exactly to the reverse, refusing to adopt the freedmen, but agreeing to the sectionizing and individualization of their domain. (See act of October 17, 1877) As one tribe cannot act without the concurrence of the other, these matters remain in statu quo. In 1889 the Chickasaw legislature amended its constitution in such a manner as to disfranchise the intermarried white citizens of the nation. This act gave rise to unpleasant complications, and is of questionable legality. The Choctaws never disfranchised their intermarried citizens. Both nations have experienced exciting times politically, and on several occasions federal intervention seemed necessary, but was happily averted. During the Overton administration in the Chickasaw Nation, forcible measures were resorted to to expel intruders and enforce the permit law; and more recently, during the Guy administration, the milita was called out to enforce the cattle tax law. The troublous incidents of the Paul-Byrd campaign are too fresh in the public mind to require more than a passing mention in this connection, as are those of the Jones-Smallwood contest in the Choctaw Nation.

GOVERNMENTAL.

The Chickasaw government is democratic in form, quite similar in its functions to the governments of states. Its relation to the federal government is anomalous and constantly giving rise to legal complications. Its power over its own citizens has of recent years become vacillating and weak.

The Chickasaw constitution is a liberal compact, declaring in favor of freedom of worship, speech, and the press; protection to person and property; equality and impartiality before the law; a fair administration of justice; equal rights and privileges to all.

The Chickasaw Nation is divided into four counties Panola, Pickens, Tishomingo and Pontotoc each county comprising a senatorial and legislative district, with five representatives and three senators from each. The senators are elected for two years and the representatives for one, the qualifications for the office being citizenship by birth, residence in the nation one year and in the county six months prior to election, the senators to be not less than thirty and the representatives not less than twenty-one years of age. The legislature meets at Tishomingo, the capital, the first Monday in September of each year. The salary of both senators and representatives is $4 per diem. The deliberations of both bodies are in accordance with the established rules of parliamentary usage, their powers being prescribed and abridged by the constitution. It requires a two-thirds vote of both branches to propose a constitutional amendment, and a two-thirds vote of both branches of the succeeding legislature to approve such proposed amendment, before it can become a part of the constitution. The legislature has power to adopt aliens as citizens. The judges of the supreme and circuit courts are elected by joint ballot of the legislature. The law-making powers of the body are based on commonly adopted principles of democratic government.

The chief executive of the nation is governor. His term of office is two years, and he is not eligible for more than two consecutive terms. He must have attained the age of thirty, be a Chickasaw by birth, and a resident of the nation one year next preceding his election. It requires a majority of all the votes cast to elect him; in the event of no majority, the legislature chooses a governor from the two candidates receiving the greatest number of votes. The salary of the governor is $1,500. Should the office become vacant, by death, or otherwise, the president of the senate acts in that capacity until the vacancy is filled by special election. The governor appoints the national secretary, the treasurer, and auditor of public accounts, besides having power of appointment in special cases. His duties and powers are generally similar to those of the same office in the states.

The judicial powers of the Chickasaw Nation are vested in a supreme court, a circuit court and county courts. The supreme court consists of a chief justice and two associates, whose term of office is four years. It meets semi-annually at the capital, the first Mondays in April and October. The supreme court has appellate jurisdiction only, under certain legislative restrictions and regulations, and original jurisdiction in extraordinary cases. The jurisdiction of the circuit court now extends over the entire nation, with its seat at Tishomingo. It holds two sessions annually, beginning the first Mondays in May and November. Original jurisdiction in all criminal cases not otherwise provided for by law, and in civil cases not cognizable before county judges, and in all matters of controversy where the amount involved exceeds $100, and exclusive original jurisdiction over felonies, is had by this court. The county courts convene the third Wednesday in each month at the county-seats of the respective counties, with jurisdiction in all matters in controversy in any sum not exceeding the value of $100. The powers of this court are similar to those of justices' courts in the states. This court is also a court of probate. The county judge is elected every two years by vote of the people, and commissioned by the governor. He has authority to open his court any day (except Sunday), for the examination of criminal cases amounting to murder, treason, felony or other misdemeanors, and to bind offenders in bond for appearance at the next term of the circuit court.

The qualifications for suffrage are these: No idiot, lunatic or criminal, and any male member of the tribe by birth, of the age of nineteen years, who has resided in the nation six months immediately prior to any election, is a qualified elector. Voting is done viva voce, not by ballot. All general elections are held on the second Wednesday in August, in each year.

EDUCATIONAL.

The school system of the Chickasaw Nation is good, the amount expended for its maintenance being exceeding large, considering the small number of those benefited. There are five boarding academies, as follows: Wappanucka (male), 60 pupils; Tishomingo (male), 60 pupils; Stonewall (female), 40 pupils; Bloomfield (female), 45 pupils; Lebanon Orphan School (male and female), 60 pupils. There are about 35 students sent to the universities of Texas and other states for higher education. For rudimentary education there are about twenty-five neighborhood schools, with an attendance of about 300 pupils. This makes the number of pupils in the nation, in all schools, 600. Allowing the ratio of one-third of the nation's citizen population (3,464) for scholastic population—a low proportion—we find that but about one-half of the children of school age are given the advantages of education. The average amount expended for those in the academies and sent abroad, is $150 per capita; for those in the neighborhood schools, (many boarding) $8 per month, or about $30,000 annually total expense of neighborhood schools. To this add $45,000 total expense of academies and scholars abroad, and we have a grand total of $75,000 devoted annually to the education of the Chickasaw youth. This is an average of $125 per annum to every pupil. It is a lamentable fact that those who should derive the most benefit from the educational system of the nation ignore, to a great degree, the opportunities offered. The full-blood element has not attained a degree of intellectual progress commensurate to the educational advantages at its command.

INTER-TRIBAL RELATIONS.

The status of Choctaws in the Chickasaw Nation, or vice versa, is this: Members of either tribe can occupy, improve and hold land in either nation, in conformity to the requirements of the tribal law, and enjoy the full protection of the government within which they reside, being amenable to the laws of the same. The 16th section of the general provisions of the Chickasaw constitution confirms the 5th article of the treaty of '55, relative to inter-tribal relations. The Chickasaws, however, fearing Choctaw domination of their affairs, took the precaution to deny Choctaws within their boundaries the privilege of suffrage or holding office. The Choctaws give the Chickasaws within the boundaries of their nation every right, privilege and immunity enjoyed by their own people. Both tribes have an equal individual interest in the lands west of the 98th meridian, commonly called the leased district. As the population of the Choctaws is about three-fourths greater than that of the Chickasaws, all monies derived from this source are divided between the tribes in the proportion of three-fourths to the former and one-fourth to the latter. All royalties arising from the development of the mineral and timber resources of either nation, are shared in the above manner. As the coal product for these nations, the past year, was 752,832 tons, valued at $1,323,806, it will be seen that this royalty is no inconsiderable sum. The Choctaws and Chickasaws, by the treaty of '55, received $800,000 for the lease of the lands west of 98° to the government, and by act of the last congress, their claim for an unqualified sale was allowed in part, an appropriation of $2,991,400 being made to extinguish their title to that part of the leased district occupied by the Cheyennes and Arapahoes. Should the full claim be allowed, they will receive an additional $3,250,000. Aside from funds arising from their mutual interest in the public domain, the Chickasaws and Choctaws have their separate annuities and interest on trust funds.

GEOGRAPHICAL.

The Choctaw and Chickasaw Nations comprise the southeast quarter of the Indian Territory, bounded on the north by the Cherokee, Creek, Seminole and Pottawatomie countries and Oklahoma Territory; on the east by Arkansas; on the south by Texas; on the west by the Kiowa, Comanche and Wichita reservations. There are 9,000,000 acres of land in the two nations. The surface is a vast rolling plain, sloping southeast. The valleys, and in many localities the hills, are timbered heavily with a variety of woods. The prairies and valleys are exceedingly fertile and naturally covered with a rank growth of nutritious grasses. Both nations are crossed by low ranges of mountains, in which are found various minerals, principally coal and iron. The temperature averages 41° winter, 75° in summer. The rain-fall will average about 45 inches. The health generally is good. The principal industries are agriculture, grazing and mining. As a producer of coal the Choctaw Nation is becoming famous, and the Chickasaw Nation likewise as a producer of cotton. The past season, although a partial crop failure was experienced, the number of bales exported was close to 40,000. Corn, wheat, oats, rye, sugar cane, millet, sorghum, tobacco, sweet and Irish potatoes, broom corn, peanuts, onions and watermelons are the chief staples. In the valleys it is not uncommon for corn and oats to make 100 bushels to the acre, and cotton one bale. Hog-raising is an important industry, mast being abundant. Cattle shipments are heavy. Peach culture, though not largely engaged in, is successfully carried on. Pecans are abundant. The area of land in cultivation is large and increasing with remarkable rapidity. The agricultural laborers are non-citizen whites, who lease their farms from the tribal citizens. There are several important towns and scores of thriving trading points in both nations, and about 80 postoffices in the Chickasaw Nation alone. Tishomingo is the Chickasaw capital and Tushkahoma the Choctaw. Ardmore is the chief city of the Chickasaw and Krebs of the Choctaw nation; among the other important towns are Purcell, Wynnewood, Minco and Paul Valley, in the former, and Atoka, Caddo and South McAlester, in the latter nation. The population of the towns is almost exclusively non-citizen. The business branches, industries and enterprises common to progressive towns in the states are to be found here. There are several flouring mills, numerous cottongins, saw mils, and also a cotton compress at Ardmore. Three railroads cross the two nations. The Santa Fe system runs north and south through the Chickasaw Nation, and the Missouri, Kansas & Texas in the same direction through the Choctaw Nation. The Choctaw Coal & Railway crosses the Choctaw Nation east and west. The terminus of the Rock Island is at present at Minco, on the northwest border of the Chickasaw Nation. Several projected roads have run their surveys through the nations. The water courses are numerous and important. The Arkansas and Canadian rivers form the north boundary and Red river the south. The Washita and Boggy are the largest interior rivers. Scores of large creeks and innumerable brooks feed the rivers. The Arkansas river is navigable to its junction with the Canadian at Webber Falls. There are no military reservations or posts in the two nations.

THE INDIAN FREEDMEN.

The Chickasaws and Choctaws have their negro question, as well as the southern states. Before the war the labor of these Indians was performed by slaves, purchased from the whites. At the date of the emancipation, the number of black bondsmen owned by the two tribes was several thousand. During the war a large per cent. of these slaves ran away from their masters, the majority going to Kansas and other free states, returning after the war and locating with their brethren who had remained upon the tribal domain. At the date of the Fort Smith treaty a great many of these negroes were not residents of the nations. The United States, desiring to provide for the future welfare of these liberated slaves, endeavored, by the treaty of '66 to have the Indians bestow certain landed rights and political privileges upon them. The conditions of these stipulations (see articles III and IV) were these: By the treaty of '55 (articles IX–X) the United States leased the lands west of 98° for the settlement of several wild tribes, paying the Choctaws and Chickasaws $800,000 for the privilege. By the treaty of '66, the federal government proposed to obtain by cession from these Indians, this leased district, for the consideration of $300,000, provided "all persons of African descent, resident in the said nations at the date of the treaty of Fort Smith, and their descendants, heretofore held in slavery among said nations [be given] all the rights, privileges and immunities, including the right of suffrage, of citizens of said nation * * * and forty acres each of the land of said nations, on the same terms as the Choctaws and Chickasaws." Should these tribes accept the above conditions, they were to receive the above amount ($300,000), "less such sum, at the rate of $100 per capita, as [should] be sufficient to pay such" freedmen as chose to permanently remove from the nations. In case the Chickasaws and Choctaws failed to carry out the foregoing stipulations within two years, it was provided that the whole $300,000 should be held for the use and benefit of such freedmen as should be removed from the territory by the United States, the United States agreeing to remove such as desired to remove, within ninety days from the expiration of the two years. If the freedmen should remain, or return after having been removed, they were to have no further interest in the $300,000, and be upon the same footing as other non-citizens, excepting that they should be entitled to as much unimproved land as is required for the support of themselves and familes. In case the Chickasaws and Choctaws should ever carry out the requirements of the treaty, the freedmen being granted citizenship should receive their allotments of forty acres of land. The Choctaws, for political artifice, adopted the freedmen residing in that nation, despite the fact that such action is not valid, according to treaty, without like action being taken by the Chickasaws. In 1876 the Chickasaw legislature, by unanimous vote, declared against the adoption of the freedmen, requesting the United States to hold the $300,000, as stipulated, and remove them beyond the limits of the nation. In 1885, the United States having failed to take action in the matter, the Chickasaw legislature again memorialized congress, requesting that the freedmen be removed to Oklahoma, and sent a delegation to Washington to lay the matter before the proper committee. The sentiment of the Chickasaws is strongly against the adoption of the negro, and that sentiment has been from time to time ingrafted in the platforms of the political parties of the nation. Without adoption by both the Choctaw and Chickasaw legislatures, there is no means by which the negro can acquire valid citizenship in these nations, the 38th article of the treaty providing only for the intermarriage of white persons and Indians. Despite the clearly defined stipulations of the treaty, the freedmen have taken possession of a large area of the best lands in both the Chickasaw and Choctaw nations, and are enjoying every landed privilege of the bona fide citizens, renting farms to both whites and negroes. As no record of the freedmen entitled to the privileges accorded by the Fort Smith treaty, has been preserved, bogus claims to interest in the public domain are the rule among the negroes. Hundreds of this class whose status is exactly that of the white non-citizens, easily evade the permit law and monopolize the public domain to the exclusion of many full-blood Indians who are compelled to occupy small and sterile patches of ground. In the Wild Horse, Caddo, and other sections of the Chickasaw Nation, there are negro landlords holding from 500 to 1,500 acres, living in affluence upon the labor of the white and black tenants. In some sections these fraudulent claimants to the rights of freedmen are leagued together for mutual protection, or rather, aggression, and hold in defiance the laws of the lands. There are instances on record where these armed usurpers have forcibly ejected Indian citizens from their claims, and resorted to Mafia methods to accomplish their nefarious ends. The Chickasaw government is powerless to correct these abuses and punish these crimes. Be it said to the discredit of the tribal authorities that up to a short time ago freedmen were allowed to obtain permits for tenants, if they, as rarely happened, chose to do so. This is in direct violation of the evident intention of the treaty of 1866. Unless the Chickasaw Nation adopts the freedmen, they will be deprived of any share in the land, under allotment. The suggestion of Hon. Sam Paul, that these freedmen memorialize congress for special allotment privileges in the Leased District, when that country is opened to settlement, is a good one and one that they will do well to act upon.

THE NON-CITIZENS.

The abolition of slavery was for many years a block to Chickasaw and Choctaw progress. Before the war such agricultural development as was done was the result of slave labor. With freedom, the ex-slaves became as indolent as the ex-masters. The plow was idle and Texas cattle companies utilized at nominal cost the rich ranges of the prairie lands. Aside from the intermarried whites, many of whom were industrious, law-abiding citizens, the class of white people who inhabited or rather sojourned in the Indian country were as a rule interlopers, stock-thieves and refugees from justice. It is easy to imagine the state of affairs under such conditions. Contact with this type of civilization did not elevate the Indian. It demoralized him. The Indian Territory and crime became synonymous. Many of the prominent citizens who prior to the war had cultivated large farms by slave labor, began to realize the necessity of a class of white farm laborers in the country. To induce farmers to settle in the nation, a permit law was passed, fixing the annual permit at twenty-five cents. The non-citizen paid the fee to his landlord and the landlord procured the permit through the county clerk, the recording fee being twenty-five cents. This law had the desired effect. Hundreds of whites began to emigrate from adjacent states and cultivate land for the Indians under a liberal system of tenancy. The Indians now began to realize that a source of wealth to themselves as individuals and a nation was to be derived from this system. Unfitted by hereditary habit and prejudice for the performance of manual labor, they perceived a simple means of gratifying their idle propensity and amassing wealth at the same time. The rich valleys were gradually cleared and put in cultivation. Log cabins and rail fences sprang up where had been a primeval wilderness. As settlements became more plentiful, the condition of the intermarried citizens and mixed-bloods improved accordingly, as they were the classes most benefited, being the most thrifty and enterprising. A great majority of the full-bloods had neither the foresight nor the energy to take advantage of the opportunities offered by the tenant system, and as a natural consequence the shrewder elements mentioned supplanted them in the possession of the common domain. About the year 1876, during the administration of Governor Overton, a radical change in the tribal policy toward non-citizens was adopted. Up to that time many thousands of cattle had been permitted to graze in the country, the foreign cattle companies evading the cattle tax law by allowing their herds to be held in the name of tribal citizens, who, of course, received fitting remuneration for this deceit. The government, being thus cheated out of its revenue, determined to correct this abuse by driving out the cattle. No revenue arising from the twenty-five cent permit fee, it was determined to raise the fee to twenty-five dollars per annum, which was done by legislative enactment. This action being deemed oppressive and unjust by the non-citizen element, many refused payment when called on for their permits. Now began a vigorous campaign on the part of the tribal government against non-permit-paying white tenants and evaders of the cattle tax law. Governor Overton was a man well fitted for carrying out aggressive measures, his hatred of the whites being equaled only by his unscrupulous cupidity. Thoroughly organizing the militia and personally directing its movements through the country, he marched from farm to farm, leaving in his track devastated homes and driving before him like so many cattle the evicted men, women and children with their stock and household effects. The majority of these "intruders," rather than be forcibly dispossessed of their homes, paid Overton the extortionate permit fee, which he appropriated for the wages of the militiamen, in direct violation of his own laws. There was no formality in these collections, many of which were never accounted for. Thousands of cattle were driven out of the country, and the majesty of tribal law was completely vindicated. About two years after this raid, the injustice of the $25 permit law became so glaring that it was amended so as to reduce the fee to $5. This reduction served to start the current of white immigration again, and the hardy pioneers of civilization began to hew them homes in the sombre forests. The discovery of coal at McAlester (1876), marked an important epoch in the progress of these nations. The development of the mines and the completion of the M. K. & T. railroad brought many non-citizen laborers to the Choctaw Nation, which in the matter of white emigration was behind the Chickasaw. Up to the date of the construction of the G. C. & S. F. railroad through the Chickasaw Nation, the development of the country was steady, but dating from that time (1887), the word most expressive of this progress is "boom." Thousands of American citizens poured into the country, allured by the prosperity of those who had gone before. They had heard of the fertile wilderness where crops could be gathered for the planting and taxation and mortgages were but memories of less favored climes. The towns which sprang up along the new railroad grew rapidly, but their pace was none too fast for the progress of the country. Now was the full-blood Indian's chance to become an independent lord of broad acres tilled by Anglo-Saxon husbandmen; but the echoes of progress, if they reached him in his forest retreat, did not awaken a responsive chord in his stolid nature. The citizens who reaped the benefits were generally those who already had as much land as they were entitled to under an equitable allotment. During the spring and summer of '88 a difficulty arose between the tribal government and many non-citizens, which for a time assumed a serious aspect. In the matter of a cattle tax the Chickasaws had gone from the extreme of $12\frac{1}{2}$ cents per annum to a law the enforcement of which meant $1 per head per month. This law was restrictive, and meant to be. Under its operation the non-citizen farmer could hold but five head of milch cows and calves, besides his oxen. As might be supposed, those whose cattle exceeded the limit disregarded the law. Governor Guy took the field with his militia to enforce the collection of the tax. He confiscated enough stock from each farmer's herd to cover the amount of tax due, and rounded them up in the vicinity of Overbrook. The farmers armed and organized for protection. The spirit which animated the "Boston Tea Party"—a sense of the injustice of taxation without representation, and resentment of oppressive discrimination—fired their hearts. A party of "rebels," under the command of Capt. George Stewart, marched to where the cattle were held by the tax collector and his posse, and with the stars and stripes floating at the head of their column, demanded the return of their stock. The collector refused the demand, and the cattle were taken by the farmers, without resistance, in the sovereign name of American citizenship. The leaders of the non-citizens were taken to Fort Smith for trial, charged with assault with intent to murder, and promptly discharged by the United States commissioner there. Some of the cattle confiscated during this raid were sold at public sale by the tribal government, as provided by the stock law, the proceeds being appropriated by the nation. The parties buying these cattle shipped them to Kansas City for market, where they were replevied and damages recovered by the lawful owners. It is said many head of cattle thus confiscated and sold were never recovered by their owners, nor was recompense made for the loss. By the representation of the Chickasaw government that a number of non-citizens were living in armed defiance of tribal law, and that bloodshed was imminent, a troop of cavalry was ordered from Fort Sill by the war department to suppress the rebellion (?). The troopers came in hot haste, expecting to participate in scenes of carnage and terror. They were happily disappointed. No phantom of war stalked abroad in the land. They stacked arms near Ardmore and joined in a grand dance and barbecue, returning in a few days to their post, crowned with the laurels of peace. The cattle tax law, from this time, was a dead letter, but it has never been repealed. No further open rupture has occurred between the tribal authorities and the alien white element, but the intruder question has for years been a bone of contention. Of late years the number of non-permit paying non-citizens has grown to many thousands. The Chickasaw Nation has been unable to enforce its permit law, and thus far all efforts in the direction of federal interference have come to naught. The only violaters of the permit law are not the non-citizens. The chief violaters are the Chickasaws themselves. If the tribal citizens would carry out the requirements of this law, the tenants on their lands could not remain without paying a permit. As no rent contract is valid for longer than one year, and a permit is one of the conditions of the lease, the renewal of such contract, when the permit condition has been disregarded, is a violation of law more flagrant on the part of the citizen than of the non-citizen. The utter abuse of their office by the permit collectors, in the manner of collections, is another example not tending to encourage the payment of permits by non-citizens. If the citizen will not exact a permit from his tenant, he should be held responsible, not the tenant. By issuing permits direct to non-citizens, and accepting from their hands the fee therefor, the collector incurs a penalty which is not enforced, and this method of procedure is the rule rather than the exception. Every man who is familiar with Chickasaw law and an observer of affairs in this nation, knows that there are two sides to this intruder question; and that the preponderance of wrong is not on the side of the non-citizen. There are, however, some non-citizens in this country who are interlopers, living in defiance of the permit law, attempting to successfully demonstrate the principle of "squatter sovereignty." These aggravated cases may require heroic treatment. On the other hand, there are some citizens living in the Chickasaw Nation who advise their tenants to ignore the permit law. The word intruder, though, as applied to non-citizens as a class who have not paid a permit fee, is a misnomer and calculated to mislead the uninformed. While the Chickasaw government has never dealt as liberally with the non-citizens as its interests would seem to justify, it is but justice to the citizens of the nation to state here that as a rule their relations with their tenants have been harmonious and to the prosperity of both. Contracts have been sacredly kept, and most of the errors made have been on the side of generosity. If the citizens, in some instances, have enriched themselves by the present system of land tenure, the non-citizens, in proportionately a much greater degree, have by the same system risen from penury to competency. It is the latter class that have made the country what it is. Without their labor there would be little land in cultivation to-day, and the cattle of Texas syndicates would dot the face of the country. Within the past four years it is safe to say that 25,000 white settlers have immigrated to the Chickasaw Nation. At this rate of increase, the problem of white invasion is one that the Indians may well ponder and act upon wisely. The development of the country and growth of the towns is phenomenal, under the circumstances. Ardmore has 2,500 inhabitants, Purcell 1,500, and many other towns several hundred. This population is exclusively non-citizen, and these people represent several millions of dollars in personal property. The proportion of the citizen to the non-citizen population in the entire nation is about 1 to 15. This state of affairs is an anomaly that will at no distant day tax the statesmanship of the Solons at Tishomingo and Washington as well.

THE PERMIT LAW.

SEC. 1. Be it enacted by the Legislature of the Chickasaw Nation, That citizens of any State or Territory of the United States, wishing to hire or rent land or be otherwise employed in this Nation, shall be required to enter into contract with a citizen, and after contract has been agreed upon, the non-citizen shall place in the hands of the citizen a sufficient amount of money to pay permits, and that the Permit Collector shall receive no permit money from any other person, except from a citizen of this Nation, and for each and every violation, shall be fined in any sum not less than ten dollars for each and every offense, by the County Judge of the county where the offense was committed.

SEC. 2. Be it further enacted, That any citizen who shall employ any non-citizen, shall apply within fifteen days after entering into contract to the Permit Collecter of the county where said non-citizen wishes to reside, for a permit for every male non-citizen over the age of eighteen years in his employ, and for each permit so obtained, the citizen shall pay to the Permit Collector issuing the same, the sum of five dollars, and the Permit Collector shall retain for each permit issued, fifteen per cent. for his services, and shall report to the Auditor and Treasurer quarterly of all monies received by him for permits, and after deducting his fee, shall pay the balance over to the Treasurer for National purposes.

SEC. 3. Be it further enacted, That every foreigner who shall come in this Nation for the purpose of farming or being otherwise employed, without the proper authority from the United States Government shall be deemed an intruder, by virtue of Section 2134 of the Revised Statues of Intercourse Law.

SEC. 4. Be it further enacted, That all licensed merchants and traders (non-citizens) shall, in addition to the tax paid on goods, be required to procure from the Permit Collector in [the county in] which they wish to trade, a permit. And all physicians [non-citizens] wishing to practice their profession, shall procure from the Governor of the Chickasaw Nation a permit, for which they shall each pay five dollars, conditioned upon the faithful observance of the laws of this Nation; and the Governor shall dispose of the funds in the manner prescribed in Section 2 of this Act.

SEC. 5. Be it further enacted, That no permit shall be granted for a longer time than twelve months, and in case of violation of any law of this Nation, the offender shall be ordered out of the limits of the Chickasaw Nation, and any citizen who shall employ any non-citizen for a longer time than fifteen days, without procuring a permit for the same, shall be deemed guilty of a misdemeanor, and be subject to a fine of twenty-five dollars, before the County Court having jurisdiction; and all fines collected under this Act shall go into the County Treasury for county purposes.

SEC. 6. Be it further enacted, That any non-citizen having entered into contract with any citizen of this Nation, and obtained a permit under his employ, and shall leave the employ of said citizen shall forfeit his permit, and no other permit shall be granted any non-citizen forfeiting the same, by either Permit Collector of this Nation.

SEC. 7. Be it further enacted, That any person living in this Nation, under permit, shall not be allowed to bring into or hold more than five head of milch cows and shall have no hogs outside of enclosure, but shall be allowed all the work horses, mules and cattle as may be necessary to work said farm and shall be allowed to feed surplus crop to beef cattle, under fence.

SEC. 8. Be it further enacted, That all freedmen not owned by the Chickasaws and Choctaws, and residing in the Nation at the date of the Treaty of Fort Smith, shall be required to get permits under citizens of the Chickasaw Nation, as other non-citizens.

SEC. 9. Be it further enacted, That any non-citizen wishing to remain in this Nation for a shorter time than twelve months can do so by paying a monthly permit to the Permit Collector, of fifty cents per month for every month or part of a month, if he wishes to reside in this Nation as mechanic or farm laborer; and that this Act is not to be construed to employ non-citizens as laborers to run stock in this Nation.

SEC. 10. Be it further enacted, That all monthly permits shall be collected as other permits, and that all Acts or parts of Acts in conflict with this Act are hereby repealed, and this Act take effect and be in force from and after its passage.

APPROVED October 17, 1876. B. F. OVERTON, Governor.

AN ACT IN REGARD TO PHYSICIANS, MECHANICS AND HOTEL MEN OBTAINING PERMITS.

SECTION 1. Be it enacted by the Legislature of the Chickasaw Nation, That if any non-citizen of the Chickasaw Nation, who wishes to practice medicine in this Nation, shall be required to get a recommendation from three resident citizens of this Nation that he is a sober man, of good moral character, and file with this recommendation a recommendation that he is a practicing physician from the board of the county and State from whence he came, and if the Governor is satisfied with said recommendation, shall issue him a permit to practice in the county and Nation, from the county he applies, upon the physician paying five dollars to the Governor, which money shall be placed in the National Treasury for National purposes, and said physician shall not charge for medicine and professional visits more than is charged in the States by regular practicing physicians.

SEC. 2. Be it further enacted, That any non-citizen who wishes to follow his trade as mechanic in the limits of this Nation, shall apply under the provision of Section first of this Act.

SEC. 3. Be it further enacted, That it shall be unlawful for any physician, mechanic or hotel man, to build or make any improvement on the public domain of the Chickasaw Nation, except licensed traders, who shall only have dwelling and business houses and lots, actually necessary to enable them to carry on their business; and any non-citizen who may have houses, lots or improvements of any kind in the limits of this Nation, shall sell or dispose of the same by the first day of January, 1888.

SEC. 4. Be it further enacted, That if any physician, mechanic or hotel men wish to practice their profession or carry on their business in the limits of this Nation, shall rent houses from some citizen of this Nation; Provided, further, That any person under provision of the first Section of this Act, desire to make any improvements on the claim of any citizen, shall first make a written contract in the presence of two witnesses, to be citizens of this Nation, and if said physicians, mechanics or hotel men fail to make said contract, as provided for by this Act, leave or vacate said place, shall forfeit all improvements made by them to the citizen owning the place.

SEC. 5. Be it further enacted, That any non-citizen refusing or failing to comply with the second Section of this Act shall be reported by any officer or citizen of this Nation to the Governor, who is hereby authorized and directed under the provision of this Act, to take such legal measures that is necessary to enforce this Act to its full intent and meaning, and any law or parts of laws coming in conflict with the provision of this Act be and the same are hereby repealed, and that this Act take effect from and after its passage.

APPROVED, September 24, 1887.

W. M. GUY, Governor.

AN ACT CREATING A PERMIT COLLECTOR IN EACH COUNTY, AND FOR OTHER PURPOSES.

SECTION 1. Be it enacted by the Legislature of the Chickasaw Nation, That at the general election in 1888 there shall be elected one Permit Collector in each County who shall serve for two years, unless sooner removed for misdemeanor in office.

SEC. 2. Be it further enacted, That before they enter on the duties of their office they shall be commissioned by the Governor, to give a good and sufficient bond in the sum of one thousand dollars to the Governor for the faithful performance of their duties, and shall receive fifteen per cent. of all the money they may collect for permits; Provided further, they shall have the right to appoint Deputy Permit Collectors, who shall give a good and sufficient bond in the sum of five hundred dollars to the Governor for the faithful discharge of his duties as Deputy Permit Collector, and for his services shall be paid by the Permit Collector out of the fifteen per cent. that he receives for his services.

SEC. 3. Be it further enacted, That the National Secretary shall furnish the Permit Collector in each county with blank certificates, book form, with stubs attached, numbered from one up, that is necessary and said stubs and certificates shall be printed and the numbers shall correspond with each other.

SEC. 4. Be it further enacted; That any parts of laws coming in conflict with the provisions of this Act is hereby repealed, and that this Act take effect from and after the general election in 1888.

APPROVED, September 23, 1887.

W. M. GUY,
Governor.

AN ACT CREATING ONE INSPECTOR OF PERMITS IN EACH COUNTY.

SECTION 1. Be it enacted by the Legislature of the Chickasaw Nation, that the Governor shall appoint one Permit Inspector in each county who shall serve to the next general election in 1888, and before he enters on the discharge of his duties shall be commissioned by the Governor and take the oath of office, that he will faithfully discharge the duties of his office.

SEC. 2. Be it further enacted, That it shall be the duty of the Inspector to take up all the permits in his county and give his receipt for the same and shall with the National Treasurer, compare the permits taken up by him with the stubs of the Permit Collector every quarter at the Capital and report all non-citizens he may find that have no permits, and it shall be the duty of the Treasurer to make a full and complete report every quarter to the Governor of his comparison with the Inspector snd Permit Collector's books and by him laid before the next Legislature.

SEC. 3. Be it further enacted, That the Inspector shall be entitled to ten per cent. out of the permit money every quarter to be paid by the Permit Collector out of the permit money he collected in the presence of the National Treasurer, and take his receipt therefor.

SEC. 4. Be it further enacted, That at the general election in 1888 each county shall elect their own Inspector for the period of two years whose duty shall be the same as provided for in this Act, and this Act take effect from and after its passage.

APPROVED, September 23, 1887.

W. M. GUY,
Governor.

The above is the permit law of the Chickasaw Nation in full, and every non-citizen in this country should study it until he is familiar with every section. By article 7 of the treaty of 1855 and article 43 of the treaty of 1866, it will be noticed that the United States gives the Choctaws and Chickasaws the right to enact legislation effecting the residence of non-citizens in their respective nations. The permit has been made the basis of such residence. Without compliance to this law, the non-citizen has no right to reside within the limits of the nation; and if the federal government is not recreant or dilatory in the performance of its duty, as defined by solemn treaty compact, it must eject violaters of the permit law from the nation as intruders. Aside from the legality of the permit law, it is but just that the non-citizens respect it. Five dollars is a very fair tax, for the privilege of a year's residence in this country. Fair-minded, law-abiding citizens of the United States who have made their homes in the Indians' country, will pay this permit tax as they would pay a tax on personal property in the states. This is the course most conducive to security and peace, and it is right.

DISFRANCHISED CITIZENS.

In accordance with the 38th article of the treaty of 1866, many white men married members of the Chickasaw tribe and have begun by amalgamation the only practical solution of the great Indian problem. Before the emigration from Mississippi, few whites had intermarried with the Chickasaws, most of those being traders and adventurers. Since that time hundreds of American citizens had gained citizenship in the Chickasaw Nation by marriage. The blending of the two races created a new era in Chickasaw affairs. The white citizens and the mixed-bloods naturally constituted the progressive elements of the tribe. It is they who have brought about, in a great measure, the agricultural development of the country. Naturally, as these classes grew in number, influence and wealth, there was a struggle for political supremacy between them and the full-blood element, who were jealous of the paler race that was rapidly supplanting them. The intermarried citizens and mixed-bloods, with a few of the more intelligent full-bloods, constituted the political organization known as the Progressive party, while the full-bloods and a few designing mixed-blood leaders constituted the National party. During the summer of 1886 a bitter, closely contested campaign was fought by the two parties, Wm. L. Byrd being the National and Wm. M. Guy the Progressive candidate for governor. Jonas Wolfe, a full-blood, ran independent for the same office. In accordance with the requirements of the constitution, no candidate having received a majority of the votes cast, the selection of governor devolved upon the legislature. The two branches of that body were pretty equally divided politically, and on joint ballot Guy won by one vote. He had led Byrd by a safe majority in the field. From the beginning of his administration, Governor Guy had to contend with a hostile legislature. The United States congress granted the Gulf, Colorado & Santa Fe railroad right of way through the Chickasaw Nation. The tribal legislature had refused to grant the charter. The full-bloods naturally regarded the railroad as a dangerous innovation, and arrayed themselves against it. When the representatives of the railroad company endeavored to negotiate with the legislature for material with which to construct their road, they were met with indifference, not to say contempt, and nothing was accomplished. The railroad company appealed to the secretary of the interior, who requested Governor Guy to call a special session of the legislature to consider the railroad's proposition. After much difficulty, the legislature was convened but instead of attending to the business demanding its attention, an effort was made to impeach the governor. As no charges could be sustained, the impeachment fell through and the legislature broke up in a disgraceful row, without considering the railroad's proposition. The secretary of the interior, when apprised of the state of affairs, ordered the governor to make the contract with the railroad company, if the legislature would not act in the matter. Governor Guy took this responsibility upon himself and collected the royalty from the company—something like $40,000. The Choctaws were given their three-fourths of this sum, but the Chickasaws refused to receive their one-fourth. In 1888 Guy was re-nominated by the Progressives and Byrd by the Nationals. The campaign which followed was the most bitter in the history of Chickasaw politics. The line between the blood and adopted citizens was tightly drawn. When the battle was over, Guy had won by 22 votes. In order to oust Guy, the legislature threw out the returns from White Bead Hill and other Guy precincts, and also the votes of Guy men in various parts of the nation, under the pretext of fraud and illegality. Immediataly after the result was declared, Byrd was sworn in as governor, and Guy and his adherents in the legislature went home. A revolution seemed imminent. The Progressives denounced the action of the legislature as a high-handed outrage and determined to seat Guy. A little band of forty or fifty fearless men hastily organized, and, armed to the teeth, they repaired to Tishomingo where the legislature was in session, led by Senator Sam Paul. Marching direct to the house of representatives, they took possession of the room, without a shot being fired. The senate, upon learning what was going on in the house, adjourned sine die, with more haste than dignity, Lem Reynolds leading the rout. Governor Byrd, who was over town at the time, was brought by an armed guard to the capitol. Mounting the speaker's platform, Senator Paul stated the object of his armed followers to be an honest count of the returns as shown by the poll books, and a determination to peaceably abide by the result of the same. "If," concluded the speaker, "William L. Byrd is found to be the lawfully elected governor of this nation, he shall serve as such; but if William M. Guy has received a majority of the votes of the people, he shall be sworn in as governor, if blood has to be spilled on the floor of this capitol." Senator Paul then demanded of the speaker of the house that he count the votes as they appeared upon the poll books. This was done, and the speaker, Ben Pikey, announced Guy's majority to be 22, and declared him the lawfully elected governor of the Chickasaw Nation. Judge Henry Duncum, of White Bead Hill, who had ridden eighty miles for that purpose, then swore in Guy as governor, in due form. Governor Guy and his body guard held the fort for several days, but as a quorum of the legislature could not be gathered to his support, he and his friends returned to their homes. Two weeks later, the pseudo governor, Byrd, quietly called his legislature together and took up the broken thread of government again, passing all the necessary appropriation bills. The legislathre, as a crowning act of infamy, refused to pay the militia which Guy had disbanded after the cattle tax trouble spoken of elsewhere in this volume. Governor Guy went to Muskogee and laid his case before the Indian agent, who referred the matter to the interior department, which in turn referred it back to the agent. The two governors were summoned before the agent and both agreed to abide by the decision of the secretary of the interior. Inasmuch as Byrd manipulated the machinery of government and was the choice of the legislature, the secretary ruled in his favor, and the matter was dropped by Guy and his friends. Now was the Byrd party's hour of revenge. At a called session of the legislature, an amendment to the constitution was proposed which would disfranchise the adopted and intermarried citizens; thus virtually annihilating the Progressive party. The intention of the constitution, in reference to an amendment, is clearly expressed in these words: "Whenever two-thirds of both branches of the legislature deem it neceseary, they may propose amendments to the constitution; and if two-thirds of both branches of the succeeding legislature approve such amendments, they shall be engrafted to and form a part of this constitution." Instead of appealing to the people through the succeeding legislative election, which is evidently meant by this section, Byrd called the same legislature in extra session again and accomplished the proposed amendment. Thus, by one stroke of legislative chicanery, a powerful opposition was completely shorn of its power, and Byrd and a coterie of his ilk were complete masters of the situation. The date of the final passage of the disfranchisement act was April 8th, 1887, several months after the amendment had been proposed. Upon learning of the proposed amendment, the inter-married citizens met in mass convention at Purcell, adopted suitable resolutions, and appointed a committee to lay their grievances before the legislature, protesting against the unconstitutionality and injustice of the contemplated act. As would be expected, little or no attention was paid to the committee. The disfranchised citizens then appealed to the interior department, but received little satisfaction from that source. Another convention was held at Ardmore, by which Hon. Sam. Paul and Judge H. F. Murray were delegated to go to Washington and lay the case before the secretary of the at least two terms of said court each year in each of the divisions aforesaid, at such regular times as said judge shall fix and determine, and shall be paid his actual traveling expenses and subsistence while attending and holding court at places other than Muskogee. And jurors for each term of said court, in each division, shall be selected and summoned in the manner provided in said act, three jury commissioners to be selected by said court for each division, who shall possess all the qualifications and perform in said division all the duties required of the jury commissioners provided for in said act. All prosecutions for crimes or offenses hereafter committed in said Indian Territory shall be cognizable within the division in which such crime or offense shall have been committed. And all civil suits shall be brought in the division in which the defendant or defendants reside or may be found; but if there be two or more defendants residing in different divisions, the action may be brought in any division in which either of the defendants resides or may be found. And all cases shall be tried in the division in which the process is returnable as herein provided, unless said judge shall direct such case to be removed to one of the other divisions: Provided, however, That the judicial tribunals of the Indian nations shall retain exclusive jurisdiction in all civil and criminal cases arising in the country in which members of the nation by nativity or by adoption shall be the only parties; and as to all such cases the laws of the State of Arkansas extended over and put in force in said Indian Territory by this act shall not apply.

SEC. 31. That certain general laws of the State of Arkansas in force at the close of the session of the general assembly of that State of eighteen hundred and eighty-three, as published in eighteen hundred and eighty-four in the volume known as Mansfield's Digest of the Statutes of Arkansas, which are not locally inapplicable or in conflict with this act or with any law of Congress, relating to the subjects specially mentioned in this section, are hereby extended over and put in force in the Indian Territory until Congress shall otherwise provide, that is to say, the provisions of the said general statutes of Arkansas relating to administration, chapter one, and the United States court in the Indian Territory herein referred to shall have and exercise the powers of courts of probate under said laws; to public administrators, chapter two, and the United States marshal of the Indian Territory shall perform the duties imposed by said chapter on the sheriffs in said State; to arrest and bail, civil, chapter seven; to assignment for benefit of creditors, chapter eight; to attachments, chapter nine; to attorneys at law, chapter eleven; to bills of exchange and promissory notes, chapter fourteen; to civil rights, chapter eighteen; to common and statute law of England, chapter twenty; to contempts, chapter twenty-six; to municipal corporations, chapter twenty-nine, division one; to costs, chapter thirty; to descents and distributions, chapter forty-nine; to divorce, chapter fifty two, and said court in the Indian Territory shall exercise the powers of the circuit courts of Arkansas under this chapter; to dower, chapter fifty-two; to evidence, chapter fifty-nine; to execution, chapter sixty; to fees, chapter sixty-three; to forcible entry and detainer, chapter sixty-seven; to frauds, statute of, chapter sixty-eight; to fugitives from justice, chapter sixty-nine; to gaming contracts, chapter seventy;

to guardians, curators. and wards, chapter seventy-three, and said court in the Indian Territory shall appoint guardians and curators; to habeas corpus, chapter seventy-four; to injunction, chapter eighty-one; to insane persons and drunkards, chapter eighty-two, and said court in the Indian Territory shall exercise the powers of the probate courts of Arkansas under this chapter; to joint and several obligations and contracts, chapter eighty-seven; to judgements and decrees, chapter eighty-eight; to judgments summary, chapter eighty-nine; to jury, chapter ninety; to landlord and tenant, chapter ninety-two; to legal notices and advertisements, chapter ninety-four; to liens chapter ninety-six; to limitations, chapter ninety-seven; to mandamus and prohibition, chapter one hundred; to marriage contracts, chapter one hundred and two; to marriages, chapter one hundred and three; to married women, chapter one hundred and four; to money and interest, chapter one hundred and nine; to mortgages, chapter one hundred and ten; to notaries public, chapter one hundred and eleven, and said court in the Indian Territory shall appoint notaries public under this chapter; to partition and sale of lands, chapter one hundred and fifteen; to pleadings and practice, chapter one hundred and nineteen; to records, chapter one hundred and twenty-six; to replevin, chapter one hundred and twenty-eight; to venue, change of, chapter one hundred and fifty-three; and to wills and testaments, chapter one hundred and fifty-five; and whenever in said laws of Arkansas the courts of record of said State are mentioned the said court in the Iddian Territory shall be substituted therefor; and whenever the clerks of said courts are mentioned in said laws the clerk of said court in the Indian Territory and his deputies, respectively, shall be substituted therefor; and whenever the sheriff of the connty is mentioned in said laws the United States marshal of the Indian Territory shall be substituted therefor, for the purpose, in each of the cases mentioned, of making said laws of Arkansas applicable to the Indian Territory.

That no attachment shall issue against improvements on real estate while the title to the land is vested in any Indian nation, except where such improvements have been made by persons, companies, or corporations operating coal or other mines, railroads, or other industries under lease or permission of law of an Indian national council, or charter, or law of the United States.

That executions upon judgments obtained in any other than Indian courts shall not be valid for the sale or conveyance of title to improvements made upon lands owned by an Indian nation, except in the cases wherein attachments are provided for. Upon a return of nulla bona, upon an execution against an adopted citizen of any Indian tribe, or against any person residing in the Indian country and not a citizen thereof, if the judgement debtor shall be the owner of any improvements upon real estate within the Indian Territory in excess of one hundred and sixty acres occupied as a homestead, such improvements may be subjected to payment of such judgment by a decree of the court in which such judgment was rendered. Proceedings to subject such property to the payment of judgments may be by petition, of which the judgment debtor shall have notice as in the original suit. If on the hearing the court shall be satisfied from the evidence that the judgment debtor is the owner of improvements on real estate, subject to the payment of said judgment, the court may order the same sold, and the proceeds, or so much thereof as may be necessary to satisfy said judgment and costs, applied to the payment of said judgment; or if the improvement is of sufficient rental value to discharge the judgment within a reasonable time the court may appoint a receiver, who shall take charge of such property and apply the rental receipts thereof to the payment of such judgment, under such regulations as the court may prescribe. If under such proceedings any improvement is sold only citizens of the tribe in which said property is situate may become the purchaser thereof.

The Constitution of the United States and all general laws of the United States which prohibit crimes and misdemeanors in any place within the sole and exclusive jurisdiction of the United States, except in the District of Columbia, and all laws relating to national banking associations shall have the same force and effect in the Indian Territory as elsewhere in the United States; but nothing in this act shall be so construed as to deprive any of the courts of the civilized nations of exclusive jurisdiction over all cases arising wherein members of said nations, whether by treaty, blood, or adoption, are the sole parties, nor so as to interfere with the right and power of said civilized nations to punish said members for violation of the statutes and laws enacted by their national councils where such laws are not contrary to the treaties and laws of the United States.

SEC. 32. That the word "county," as used in any of the laws of Arkansas which are put in force in the Indian Territory by the provisions of this act, shall be construed to embrace the territory within the limits of a judicial division in said Indian Territory; and whenever in said laws of Arkansas the word "county" is used, the words "judicial division" may be substituted therefor, in said Indian Territory, for the purposes of this act. And whenever in the said laws of Arkansas the word "State" or the words "State of Arkrnsas," are used, the word "Territory" or the words "Indian Territory," may be substituted therefor, for the purposes of this act, and for the purpose of making said laws of Arkansas applicable to the said Indian Territory; but all prosecutions therein shall run in the name of the "United States."

SEC. 33. That the provisions of chapter forty-five of the said general laws of Arkansas, entitled "Criminal Law," except as to the crimes and misdemeanors mentioned in the provisos to this section, and the provisions of chapter forty-six of said general laws of Arkansas, entitled "Criminal Proceedure," as far as they are applicable, are hereby extended over and put in force in the Indian Territory, and jurisdiction to enforce said provisions is hereby conferred upon the United States court herein. Provided, That in all cases where the laws of the United States and the said criminal laws of Arkansas have provided for the punishment of the same offenses the laws of the United States shall govern as to such offenses: And provided further, That the United States circuit and district courts, respectively, for the western district of Arkansas and the eastern district of Texas, respectively shall continue to exercise exclusive jurisdiction as now provided by law in the

Indian Territory as defined in this act, in their respective districts as heretofore established, over all crimes and misdemeanors against the laws of the United States applicable to the said Territory, which are punishable by said laws of the United States by death or by imprisonment at hard labor, except as otherwise provided in the following sections of this act.

SEC. 34. That original jurisdiction is hereby conferred upon the United States court in the Indian Territory to enforce the provisions of title twenty-eight, chapters three and four, of the Revised Statutes of the United States in said Territory, except the offenses defined and embraced in sections twenty-one hundred and forty-two and twenty-one hundred and forty-three: Provided, That as to the violations of the provisions of section twenty-one hundred and thirty-nine of said Revised Statutes, the jurisdiction of said court in the Indian Territory shall be concurrent with the jurisdiction exercised in the enforcement of such provisions by the United States courts for the western district of Arkansas and the eastern district of Texas. Provided, That all violations of said chapters three and four, prior to the passage of this act, shall be prosecuted in the said United States courts, respectively, the same as if this act had not been passed.

SEC. 35. That exclusive original juriseiction is hereby conferred upon the United States court in the Indian Territory to enforce the provisions of chapter four, title seventy, of the Revised Statutes of the United States entitled "Crimes against justice," in all cases where the the crimes mentioned therein are committed in any judicial proceeding in the Indian Territory and where such crimes affect or impede the enforcement of the laws in the courts established in said Territory: Provided, That all violations of the provisions of said chapter prior to the passage of this act shall be prosecuted in the United States courts for the western district of Arkansas and the eastern district of Texas, respectively, the same as if this act had not been passed.

SEC. 36. That jurisdiction is hereby conferred upon the United States court in the Indian Territory over all controversies arising between members or citizens of one tribe or nation of Indians and the members or citizens of other tribes or nations in the Indian Territory, and any citizen or member of one tribe or nation who may commit any offense or crime against the person or property of a citizen or member of another tribe or nation shall be subject to the same punishment in the Indian Territory as he would be if both parties were citizens of the United States. And any member or citizen of any Indian tribe or nation in the Indian Territory shall have the right to invoke the aid of said court therein for the protection of his person or property as against any person not a member of the same tribe or nation, as though he were a citizen of the United States.

SEC. 37. That if any person shall, in the Indian Territory, open, carry on, promote, make or draw, publicly or privately, any lottery, or scheme of chance of any kind or description, by whatever name, style or title the same may be denominated or known, or shall, in said Territory, vend, sell, barter or dispose of any lottery ticket or tickets, order or orders, device or devices, of any kind, for, or representing any number of shares or any interest in any lottery or scheme of chance, or shall open or establish as owner or otherwise any lottery or scheme of chance in said Territory, or shall be in any wise concerned in any lottery or scheme of chance, by acting as owner or agent in said Territory, for or on behalf of any lottery or scheme of chance, to be drawn, paid or carried on, either out of or within said Territory, every such person shall be deemed guilty of a misdemeanor, and, on conviction thereof, shall be fined for the first offense, not exceeding five hundred dollars, and for the second offense shall, on conviction, be fined not less than five hundred dollars and not exceeding five thousand, and he may be imprisoned, in the discretion of the court, not exceeding one year. And jurisdiction to enforce the provisions of this section is hereby conferred upon the United States court in said Indian Territory, and all persons therein, including Indians and members and citizens of Indian tribes and nations, shall be subject to its provisions and penalties.

SEC. 38. The clerk and deputy clerks of said United States court shall have the power within their respective divisions to issue marriage licenses or certificates and to solemnize marriages. They shall keep copies of all marriage licenses or certificates issued by them, and a record book in which shall be recorded all licenses or certificates after the marriage has been solemnized, and all persons authorized by law to solemnize marriages shall return the license or certificate, after executing the same, to the clerk or deputy clerk who issued it, together with his return thereon. They shall also be ex-officio recorders within their respective divisions, and as such they shall perform such duties as are required of recorders of deeds under the said laws of Arkansas, and receive the fees and compensation therefor which are provided in said laws of Arkansas for like service; Provided, That all marriages heretofore contracted under the laws or tribal customs of any Indian nation now located in the Indian Territory are hereby declared valid, and the issue of such marriages shall be deemed legitimate and entitled to all inheritances of property or rights, the same as in the case of the issue of other forms of lawful marriage: Provided further, That said chapter one hundred and three of said laws of Arkansas shall not be construed so as to interfere with the operation of the laws governing marriage enacted by any of the civilized tribes, nor to confer any authority upon any officer of said court to unite a citizen of the United States in marriage with a member of any of the civilized nations until the preliminaries to such marriage shall have first been arranged according to the laws of the nation of which said Indian person is a member: And provided further, That where such marriage is required by law of an Indian nation to be of record, the certificate of such marriage shall be sent for record to the proper officer, as provided in such law enacted by the Indian nation.

SEC. 39. That the United States court in the Indian Territory shall have all the powers of the United States circuit courts or circuit court judges to appoint commissioners within said Indian Territory, who shall be learned in the law, and shall be known as United States commissioners; but not exceeding three commissioners shall be appointed for any one division, and such commissioners when appointed shall have, within the district to be designated in the order appointing them, all the powers of commissioners of circuit courts of the United

States. They shall be ex officio notaries public, and shall have power to solemnize marriages. The provisions of chapter ninety-one of the said laws of Arkansas, regulating the jurisdiction and proceedure before justices of the peace, are hereby extended over the Indian Territory; and said commissioners shall exercise all the powers conferred by the laws of Arkansas upon justices of the peace within their districts; but they shall have no jurisdiction to try any cause where the value of the thing or the amount in controversy exceeds one hundred dollars.

Appeals may be taken from the final judgment of said commissioners to the United States court in said Indian Territory in all cases and in the same manner that appeals may be taken from the final judgments of justices of the peace under the provisions of said chapter ninety-one. The said court may appoint a constable for each of the commissioner's districts designated by the court, and the constable so appointed shall perform all the duties required of constables under the provision of chapter twenty-four and other laws of the State of Arkansas. Each commissioner and constable shall execute to the United States, for the security of the public, a good and sufficient bond, in the sum of five thousand dollars, to be approved by the judge appointing him, conditioned that he will faithfully discharge the duties of his office and account for all moneys coming into his hands, and he shall take an oath to support the Constitution of the United States and to faithfully perform the duties required of him.

The appointments of United States commissioners by said court held at Muscogee, in the Indian Territory, heretofore made, and all acts in pursuance of law and in good faith performed by them, are hereby ratified and validated.

SEC. 40. That persons charged with any offense or crime in the Indian Territory, and for whose arrest a warrant has been issued, may be arrested by the United States marshal or any of his deputies, wherever found in said Territory, but in all cases the accused shall be taken, for preliminary examination, before the commissioner in the judicial division whose office or place of business is nearest by the route usually traveled to the place where the offense or crime was committed; but this section shall apply only to crimes or offenses over which the courts located in the Indian Territory have jurisdiction: Provided, That in all cases where persons have been brought before a United Stares commissioner in the Indian Territory for preliminary examination, charged with the commission of any crime therein, and where it appears from the evidence that a crime has been committed, and that there is probable cause to believe the accused guilty thereof, but that the crime is one over which the courts in the Indian Territory have no jurisdiction, the accused shall not, on that account, be discharged, but the case shall be proceeded with as provided in section ten hundred and fourteen of the Revised Statutes of the United States.

SEC. 41. That the judge of the United States court in the Indian Territory shall have the same power to extradite persons who have taken refuge in the Indian Territory, charged with crimes in the States or other Territories of the United States, that may now be exercised by the governor of Arkansas in that State, and he may issue requisitions upon governors of States and other Territories for persons who have committed offenses in the Indian Territory, and who have taken refuge in such States or Territories.

SEC. 42. That appeals and writs of error may be taken and prosecuted from the decisions of the United States court in the Indian Territory to the Supreme Court of the United States in the same manner and under the same regulations as from the circuit courts of the United States, except as otherwise provided in this act.

SEC. 43. That any member of any Indian tribe or nation residing in the Indian Territory may apply to the United States court therein to become a citizen of the United States, and such court shall have jurisdiction thereof and shall hear and determine such application as provided in the statutes of the United States; and the Confederated Peoria Indians residing in the Quapaw Indian Agency, who have heretofore or who may hereafter accept their land in severalty under any of the allotment laws of the United States, shall be deemed to be, and are hereby, declared to be citizens of the United States from and after the selection of their allotments, and entitled to all the rights, privileges, and benefits as such, and parents are hereby declared from that time to have been and to be the legal guardians of their minor children without process of court: Provided, That the Indians who become citizens of the United States under the provisions of this act do not forfeit or lose any rights or privileges they enjoy or are entitled to as members of the tribe or nation to which they belong.

SEC. 44. That the following sum, or so much thereof as may be necessary, is hereby appropriated, out of any money in the Treasury not otherwise appropriated, to be disbursed under the direction of the Attorney-General of the United States, in the same manner that similar appropriations are disbursed in the other Territories of the United States, namely:

To pay the actual traveling and other expenses of the judge of the United States court holding court in said Indian Territory other than at Muskogee; to pay for the rent of buildings for the court; to provide jails and support prisoners; to pay mileage and per diem of jurors and witnesses; to provide books, records, and stationery for the judicial offices for the remainder of the fiscal year ending June thirtieth, eighteen hundred and ninety, the snm of ten thousand dollars.

APPROVED, May 2, 1890.

THE U. S. COURT.

The United States government has always asserted its jurisdiction over the Indian country, and in all the treaties made with the innumerable tribes and nations of Indians with whom it has dealt, and in all the statutes passed to carry the treaties into effect, its dominion over them has been made prominent and unmistakable. Following the example of the European powers who planted colonies in America before the Revolution, the United States for nearly a century has recognized in the Indian tribes or nations competency to contract with the United States by treaty, regarding them as independent communities, subject to the government of the United States. But in 1871 congress passed an act now embodied in section 2079 of the United States Revised Statutes, which reads as follows:

"No Indian nation or tribe within the territory of the United States shall be acknowledged or recognized as an independent nation, tribe or power with whom the United States may contract by treaty. But no obligation of any treaty lawfully made and ratified with any such Indian nation or tribe prior to March 3d, 1871, shall be hereby invalidated."

That statute is still in full force. In the United States vs. Kagama, 118 U. S. Statutes, p. 375, the United States Supreme Court, referring to the Indians in former decisions of that court said: "In the opinions in these cases they are spoken of as wards of the nation, pupils or local dependent communities." In this spirit the United States has conducted its relations to them from its organization to this time. But after an experience of a hundred years of the treaty-making system of government congress has determined upon a new departure—to govern them by act of congress. Since that time the United States has made no treaties with the Indians. Commissions have been appointed to negotiate with different tribes or nations in regard to the sale of lands, such as the commission appointed to negotiate for the purchase of the Cherokee Strip, but no treaties have been made. It is now the settled policy of the United States, not to recognize any nation or tribe of Indians as being competent to cantract with the United States by treaty.

In the treaties between the United States and the five civilized nations the right to punish their own citizens for violations of their own laws is secured to the Indians. Article thirty-eight of the treaty of 1866 between the United States and the Choctaw and Chickasaw Indians reads as follows: "Every white person who having married a Choctaw or Chickasaw, resides in the Choctaw or Chickasaw Nations, or who has been adopted by the legislative authorities, is to be deemed a member of said nations, and shall be subject to the laws of the Choctaw or Chickasaw Nations, according to his domicile, and to prosecution and trials before their tribunals and to punishment according to their laws in all respects as though he was a native Choctaw or Chickasaw." This article of the treaty confers on the courts of the Choctaw and Chickasaw Nations jurisdiction over the citizens of those nations by adoption or intermarriage. Similar provisions are contained in the treaties between the United States and the Seminole and Cherokee Nations. But the jurisdiction of the Indian courts is strictly confined to crimes committed by one citizen or member of an Indian tribe or nation against the person or property of another citizen or member of such tribe or nation of Indians. If a citizen or member of a nation or tribe of Indians commit an offense against the person or property of a person not a citizen of such tribe or nation, the Indian courts have no jurisdiction; or, if an offense be committed by a person not a citizen or member of a nation or tribe of Indians against the person or property of a citizen or member of such tribe or nation, the Indian courts have no jurisdiction. In all such cases the jurisdiction is vested exclusively in the United States courts. Sections 2145 and 2146 Revised Statutes of the United States, read as follows:

SEC. 2145. "Except as to crimes the punishment of which is expressly provided for in the title the general laws of the United States as to the punishment of crimes in any place within the sole and exclusive jurisdiction of the United States except in the District of Columbia, shall extend to the Indian country."

SEC. 2146. "The preceeding section shall not be construed to extend to crimes committed by one Indian against the person or property of another Indian, nor to any Indian committing any offense in the Indian country who has been punished by the local law of the tribe, or to any case where, by treaty stipulations, the exclusive jurisdiction over such offenses is or may be secured to the Indian tribe respectively."

Besides the general laws of the United States providing for the punishment of crime, by act of congress, approved May 2, 1890, the general laws of the State of Arkansas, providing for the punishment of crimes, were extended over and put in effect in the Indian Territory. There is now in force as full and complete a system of criminal laws as can be found in any of the states, but the efficiency of the system is generally impaired by the fact that for most of the graver offenses the accused is transported beyond the limits of the Territory and tried in the United States district courts at Fort Smith, Ark., and Paris, Tex. The Fort Smith and Paris courts have jurisdiction of all offenses where the penalty fixed by the law of the United States is confinement in the penitentiary for more than one year, this includes assault to murder, and horse theft, and all offenses of a higher grade. Offenses of this character committed in the Quapaw Indian Agency, the Creek Nation, Cherokee Nation, and the northern part of the Choctaw Nation, are punishable in the Ft. Smith court; those committed in the Chickasaw Nation, the Seminole Nation, and the southern part of the Choctaw Nation, in the Paris court. All other offenses punishable by the laws of the United States, including theft of cattle, aggravated assault, etc., are within the jurisdiction of the United States courts for the Indian Territory. These courts also have jurisdiction, regardless of the grade, of all offenses punishable by the laws of the state of Arkansas now in force in the Territory that are not punishable by the laws of the United States. The courts in the Territory also have concurrent jurisdiction with the Fort Smith and Paris courts in the enforcement of the laws prohibiting the introduction and sale of intoxicating liquors in the Territory.

If a man is charged with stealing a horse worth ten dollars he may be taken to Paris for trial. If he is charged with stealing a hundred head of beef steers, worth $3,000, or more, he may be tried at Ardmore. That the jurisdiction now exercised by the Fort Smith and Paris courts over the Indian Territory ought to be discontinued and vested in the United States courts in the Indian Territory is admitted by everybody except the few who profit by the divided jurisdiction. The great distance that prisoners and witnesses are compelled to travel to the Fort Smith and Paris courts, make those courts enormously expensive to the government and inconvenient to the people. But this is only a trifling objection. The practice of transporting prisoners from the Territory for trial in Arkansas and Texas involves a vicious principle. One of the acts of tyranny charged against George III, in the Declaration of Independence, is that he gave his assent to legislation "for transporting us beyond the sea to be tried for pretended offenses." Every intelligent community ought to try its own criminals, and be held responsible before the world for their conviction or acquittal. No people on earth are better qualified to try their own criminals than the people of the Indian Territory.

The last census shows that there are 107,000 white people in the five civilized nations. These people are industrious, lawabiding and intelligent; they have driven away the cattle-herder and converted the praries and forests into productive farms of corn, wheat and cotton; they have sunk shafts into the earth and taken therefrom millions of dollars worth of coal, and opened the way to untold mineral treasures; they have built railroads, towns and cities; they have planted the standard of American civilization in the rich soil of the Indian Territory, and are supporting it with that enterprise and spirit which has marked the progress of the same people throughout the United States.

Congress has at last awakened to the necessity of conferring on the courts established among these people, complete criminal jurisdiction, and the Attorney-General has recommended it. It will only require united action on the part of the people to induce Congress to grant it. Prior to March 1, 1889, none but the Indian courts had civil jurisdiction in the Indian Territory, and they, of course, took cognizance only of controversies between Indian citizens. There were, perhaps, 70,000 white people and no courts with civil jurisdiction. Many men had brought property into the Territory to avoid paying debts; many had come to the Territory where they would be beyond the reach of their creditors until they could rebuild broken fortunes. The commercial interests of the people were rapidly expanding, and wholesale merchants, who sold goods to local dealers, were without means of enforcing payment. Congress after Congress was appealed to for courts of civil jurisdiction. The Indians bitterly opposed such a court and did all they could, through their well paid lobby in Washington, to prevent its establishment. But by act, approved March 1, 1889, the United States court was established at Muskogee, the sixth section of which act reads as follows:

SEC. 6. That the court hereby established shall have jurisdiction in all civil cases between citizens of the United States who are residents in the Indian Territory, or between citizens of the United States, or of any state or territory therein, and any citizen or person or persons residing or found in the Indian Territory, and whenever the value of the thing in controversy, or damages or wrong claimed, shall amount to one hundred dollars or more: Provided, that nothing herein shall be so construed as to give the court jurisdiction over controversies between persons of Indian blood only.

Under the authority of this section the court entertained civil suits of evey character except those wherein the only parties are Indians by blood. Indians by adoption or intermarriage sued Indians by blood and vice versa, ad infinitum. The docket of the court soon became overcrowded. The great extent of the territory under jurisdiction of the court, covering the entire Indian Territory, Oklahoma and No Man's Land, made litigation to distant parties, extremely burdensome. By act of May 2, 1890, published in full in this book, begining on page 41, additional courts were created at South McAlister and at Ardmore, restricting the territorial jurisdiction to the Quapaw Indian agency and the five civilized nations, and putting in operation therein all that could be made applicable of the civil code and laws of the State of Arkansas. This act provided that the courts in the Indian Territory should have all the jurisdiction conferred on the United States court at Muskogee, by the act of March 1, 1889, and after conferring jurisdiction to enforce the laws of Arkansas, put in operation therein, the latter part of section thirty contains the following proviso: "Provided, however, that the judicial tribunals of the Indian Nations shall retain exclusive jurisdiction in all civil and criminal cases arising in the couuntry in which members of the nation, by nativity or by adoption, shall be the only parties, and as to all such cases the laws of the State of Arkansas extended over and put in operation in said Indian Territory by this act shall not apply."

This provision was construed by many able lawyers as a limitation on the jurisdiction of the courts of the Indian Territory, so as to exclude therefrom all cases wherein the only parties were citizens of an Indian ation by blood, adoption or intermarriage. The point arose for the first time in the celebrated case of Roff and Watkins vs. Richard McLish, tried at the March term, 1891, at Ardmore. Roff and Watkins both claimed to be citizens of the Chickasaw Nation by intermarriage, and that McLish was a Chickasaw citizen by blood. McLish interposed a plea to the jurisdiction of the court, on the ground that the only parties to the suit were citizens of the Chickasaw Nation, and that the Chickasaw tribunals had exclusive jurisdiction. But Judge Shackleford overruled the plea, holding that his court had jurisdiction over all controversies between Indian citizens by intermarriage and citizens of any Indian nation by blood or adoption. This is important to the intermarried citizens because they will not be compelled to litigate their rights in the Indian courts, where blind prejudice against the whites, instead of the blind goddess of justice, presides. In that case another point of interest to everybody was decided. That is a United States citizen who married a citizen of an Indian nation, and thereby became a citizen of such nation, did not by virtue of that fact, cease to be a citizen of the United States. In this Judge Shackleford followed rules laid down by the Supreme Court of the United States vs. Wm. Rogers, 45, U. S., p. 567, decided in 1846, and adhered to ever since. The United States citizens who have married Indian citizens, become members and citizens of the Indian Nation, as provided in the thirty-eight article of the treaty of 1866. but are still citizens of the United States.

Section forty-three of the act of March 2, 1890, reads as follows: "That any member of any Indian tribe or nation residing in the Indian Territory, may apply to the United States court therein to become a citizen of the United States, and such court shall have jurisdiction thereof, and shall hear and determine such application as provided in the statutes of the United States. * * * Provided, That the Indians who become citizens of the United States, under the provisions of this act, do not forfeit or lose any right or privilege they enjoy, or are entitled to, as members of the Tribe or Nation to which they belong." Under this provision many Indian citizens by blood, adoption and intermarriage have taken the naturalization oath and become citizens of the United States. As to adopted or intermarried citizens this is but an empty form. If they were United States citizens when they were adopted, or married into an Indian tribe, and did not lose their United States citizenship, by taking the oath they acquire nothing. The evident and only object of this provision is to encourage Indians by blood to become citizens of the United States.

ALLOTMENT.

The community of land system of the five civilized tribes of the Indian Territory furnishes a unique feature of the Indian question which at this juncture demands the best statesmanship and considera tion of the federal and tribal governments and the people mostly directly interested. Here is an anomaly that challenges the attention of the American people. The longer it is allowed to exist, the more difficult will be the complications that arise to perplex an equitable solution of the problem. Already the evil has taken too firm a root to be eradicated by summary and severe measures. Reform can only be justly accomplished by a spirit of moderation and compromise.

The United States government is largely responsible for the existing state of affairs. By the treaty of 1866 it needlessly bound its hands by making certain provisions optional instead of compulsory on the part of the Choctaws and Chickasaws. Had the federal government so demanded, the allotment of the lands of these tribes in severalty would have been accomplished shortly after the civil war. The government, in article XI of the treaty, realized "that the holding of said land in severalty will promote the general civilization of said nations, and tend to advance their permanent welfare and the best interests of their individual members," and desired that these nations abolish the community system of land tenure. The manner of allotment was given in every detail, and the framers of the treaty no doubt expected that this provision would be carried out to the letter; but as the Indian governments were not bound to accept the desired change, their lands, after a quarter of a century of civilization, are held in common, and the unfortunate results of the system are constantly becoming more manifest.

The intention of the United States in granting the Choctaws and Chickasaws a patent to their lands, was to benefit all the tribal members alike, so far as their interest in the common domain is concerned. The conditions which now exist could not have been foreseen at that time. Had these people been equally intelligent, enterprising and wealthy, their chances under the community system of holding the land would have been equal, but there are many things to be taken into con sideration in this connection. Before the emigration from Mississippi, the work of amalgamation between the two races had begun. Since the war the diffusion of white blood has become general. The intermarried whites and their children naturally comprise the progressive elements of the tribe. Greed of gain is not an Indian characteristic. The simple full-bloods were content to occupy a small acreage of the common domain, their lives undisturbed by avariciousness and their wants few. Not so the intermarried whites and mixed-bloods. The system of land tenure afforded them monopolistic opportunities which they were not slow to take advantage of. As a consequence, the lands of the Chickasaw Nation have practically passed from the hands of the Indian. Where one hundred acres are controlled by the full-bloods, ten thousand acres are controlled by the intermarried whites. As immigration increases, the rights of the full-blood are more and more circumscribed, and the wealth and power of the adopted citizens and mixed-bloods is increased accordingly. Under existing conditions, the full-blood has been robbed of his birthright, and his blood in the veins of the white man is weighed with apothecary's scales. When his children have reached the age when they should make homes of their own, they find the desirable portions of their heritage in the possession of the usurper, and are crowded to the wilderness yet unclaimed by their more enterprising fellow citizens, while the children of the latter class, through their parents or guardians, control much of the most valuable land in the country.

A system of tenancy incompatible with the spirit of American institutions and a standing disgrace to the government's mistaken Indian policy, is the natural outgrowth of the land tenure of the Chickasaw Nation. Here is an interesting study in the philosophy of civilization. Fifty thousand people in whose veins flows pure Anglo-Saxon blood, the tenants of less than four thousand Indians (so-called). There are but several hundred full-bloods in the Chickasaw Nation. Including these, the tribe will average as high in intelligence and business capability as an equal number of American citizens selected indiscriminately from any agricultural community in the west. Here is class discrimination with a vengeance. The few allowed to monopolize a vast area of arable land, without individual title to earth enough for a grave, while the alien many have not even the security of a lease which the law of the land will recognize as valid for longer than one year, after years of toil and expense in developing the country and erecting improvements. As an example of the workings of this system, here is a white man who has married a woman of one-sixteenth Indian blood. He has fenced in ten thousand acres of the tribal domain, which he rents by the acre, or for a share of the crops, to several hundred non-citizen whites, and lives in affluence and amasses wealth from the labor of his tenantry. Near him, upon a patch of ground comprising less than fifty acres, his dwelling a hovel and his simplest wants with difficulty supplied, lives a full-blood Indian, the one above all others meant to be benefited by the domain patented to his fathers by the United States. Wealth is the portion of the one, poverty of the other. The wealthy tribal citizen has no more interest in this land than the poor Indian, but because he is wealthy he can monopolize the full-blood's share. We boast of our civilization and the eternal fitness of republican institutions, but this boast is Pharisaical when applied to the government's policy toward its civilized Indians.

Under the land system of these civilized tribes, the federal government is maintaining on a colossal scale a system of white peonage which Americans would point to as an evil of monarchal government, were the instance in Russia instead of the United States.

The men who have reaped the benefits of the community of land, have moulded the tribal government to suit their interests, and the full-blood is an unconscious instrument in their hands to further their cunning designs. So long as less than a dozen white men with Indian hatreds control the entire machinery of government, constituting as they do a petty oligarchy, there is little hope of a movement looking to a change in the land tenure from a system of community to severalty, having its origin or support from such an source. If these men could rise above the narrow ruts of selfishness, avariciousness, obstinacy and prejudice, to the broad plane of patriotism and statesmanship, as befits the exigency of the times, the desired change would be easily effected, and generations yet unborn would laud their action. Nothing short of federal interference or a political revolution among the Chickasaw people, will bring about the end imperatively demanded by existing conditions in this nation.

It is hard to discuss this allotment question from a standpoint of absolute justice. There are so many conflicting interests to harmonize, so many race prejudices to overcome, so many enmities to conciliate, so many differences of opinion as to the manner of effecting the result, that an attempt to satisfy even a considerable majority of all the people effected in one way or another, would be almost futile. That the time has come when this question must be discussed publicly, with the principle of equity to those most vitally interested paramount, is acknowledged by all fair-minded men. The situation, on whatever hand we may view it, is neither inviting nor pleasant; but between two evils, the wise plan is to choose the lesser. There are those who would delay the early consummation of allotment through selfish motives. This is natural, but not politic. The last two years have brought about circumstances in the Indian Territory which force this question upon the consideration of the Indian people as a matter of self-protection. There are two opposing elements when allotment is broached, among both citizens and non-citizens. Those who favor immediate and decisive action in the matter, realize that delay will but aggravate existing complications, and that what is inevitable had best be brought about at once. They are building for the future, conscious of the moment of the cause which they espouse, and are willing to make temporary personal sacrifices for the benefits which will accrue to themselves and their children from a permanent land tenure. Those who favor procrastination are working on the theory that the morrow will take care of itself, without concerning to-day. They are unwilling to make sacrifices for the general good and for posterity, selfishly clinging to the hope that their opposition will impede the irresistible trend of events toward the only practical solution—allotment.

However much we may desire present conditions to continue, because we are peculiarly benefited thereby, the fact should not be lost sight of that the natural law of change is inexorable, and that individuals are but wooden puppets in the hands of the destinies which shape this shifting world. We may cry out against seemingly needless innovations, and bruise our rebellious bodies in a mad attempt to block the path of progress, but our puny strength were better not expended against omnipotence. Civilization is remorseless as death. The weak must succumb to the strong. There is no room for sentimentality in the harsh doctrine of the survival of the fittest. The tide of progress has penetrated to the remotest forests and deserts of this continent. It has dashed into the very heart of the Indian Territory. It threatens to inundate every acre of the land. Every effort of the civilized Indian to hold it back is but a bulwark of sand against the flood-tide of popular clamor. The higher he builds, the stronger is the pressure of the current. He can stand behind this imaginary defense to-day, but let him beware of the time when the chafing, surging breakers level the last vestige of the dam and leave him floating on the ebb-tide of his folly.

Since the day has passed when allotment can be considered but as a bugaboo of the vague future, to be shifted upon the shoulders of coming generations, let us look the question squarely in the face and recognize the fact that to-day it is the one living issue among the five civilized tribes. Conditions as strained as those which confront our every day life cannot be lightly regarded. As the tension increases, the danger of a break is imminent. It is wisdom to fortify against impending evil. As the Chickasaw people are the chief parties interested, being the sole owners of the land, it is fitting that they inaugurate this crying reform in their land tenure, without waiting for the strong arm of the federal government to be interposed further in their affairs. While the non-citizens who have built homes upon their domain must recognize the fact that they have little else than a moral right to demand liberal treatment at the hands of the Indians, under the changed land tenure, the latter class would be utterly lost to all sense of justice, if concessions were not made in the way of respecting non-citizen claims to improvements throughout the nation. While no lease is recognized by tribal law for longer than one year, and tenants are in reality at the mercy of their landlords as matters stand to-day, thousands of non-citizens are cultivating farms under contracts binding upon the honor of the citizens, many of these contracts covering a long term of years. Aside from leniency in this matter, which ought to be satisfactorily adjusted by mutual compromise, the Indian citizens have the disposition of the allotment question in their own hands and should deal with it as becomes an intelligent, patriotic, honorable people.

As to the manner of allotment, that is open to a wide range of discussion. The allotment provisions of the treaty of 1866, with modifications in accord with present conditions and present sentiment, might be profitably taken as a basis of operations. The general desire of the Chickasaw people seems to be an equal apportionment of the national domain among all the tribal citizens, with the exception of reservations for school purposes, townsites and public highways. An equal division of the lands of the Choctaw and Chickasaw Nations among every man, woman and child in the two tribes, with exceptions as above stated, would give each an allotment of at least 600 acres. A quarter section of this apportionment should be reserved in a body as a homestead for each citizen, inalienable for a proper term of years, with adequate safeguards for minors and incompetents. In the case of the full-bloods, some of whom it is alleged are not capable of protecting their interests after receiving their pro rata share, a larger acreage might be made inalienable, subject to the discretion of a board of trustees, every precaution being taken to avoid unjust discrimination. To insure absolute impartiality in the division of the land, and at the same time work few hardships upon citizens owning valuable improvements, would necessitate an elaborate system of surveys and a thorough land office service. For instance, a faithful chart or map should be drawn from the surveys, showing the exact character of every acre of land in the country to be allotted, the same to be classified under the general heads of prairie, valley, grazing, timber, mineral and desert lands. Aside from the homestead reservations of 160 acres, which should include the land surrounding or immediately contiguous to the residences of claimants as their first choice, with the privilege of a like selection for their wards, the remainder of each citizen's pro rata should be parceled in tracts of not less than forty acres, according to the classification of the same, with the privilege of first choice should such classified land lie adjacent to homestead tracts. By this manner of division, many citizens would be able to hold the bulk of their allotment in one body, especially when guardians of minors, and only those who have monopolized an exorbitant area of the common domain would be compelled to surrender a portion of their claims to their less fortunate fellow citizens. The details of the duties of the land office, as set forth in various articles of the treaty, and in fact the general allotment provisions, would require but little modification to suit the requirements of the times. Article XXIV, which applies to townsites, is useful in the present dilemma only as a suggestion to the tribal government that some provision for townsites is imperative with or without allotment. At the time this treaty was made, the non-citizen did not figure prominently as a feature of the townsite case, but to-day his interest is by far the chief one concerned, and complications at that time unconsidered, if not unforseen, have arisen to perplex the status of this question. However, there is nothing in an equitable solution of the townsite problem which will seriously effect the fair and speedy accomplishment of allotment. Many features of the townsite law as applied in the settlement of Oklahoma, would be applicable in the adjustment of townsites in the Indian Territory. From the sale of town lots to non-citizens, the Chickasaws would derive a revenue, which, added to the rever derived from school lands, would create an handsome fund for educational or governmental purposes. Under article XLVII of the treaty, provision is made for the withdrawal of the invested fund held in trust by the United States, the amount thereof to be equally divided and paid per capita to the tribal members. Should the Chickasaws so desire, all their available funds could be thus disbursed. This money, together with the receipts from the sale of the leased district, would place the Chickasaw people upon a solid financial basis individually, and especially would it benefit the full bloods who have accumulated little of this world's goods under more than half a century of the present land system.

After the lands of the Chickasaws have been individualized and patents issued to the lawful claimants from the United States, the relations between the land owners and the tenant class would be practically the same in cases where citizens were able to control their former holdings. Where tenants were compelled to change landlords, their leased farms becoming the property of another under allotment, it is not probable that they would be subjected to injustices greater than under the present system. There seems to be no foundation for the plaint of a certain element that allotment will disrupt and confuse the entire land tenure of the nation, working severe hardships upon nearly the entire population, citizens and non-citizens. The spirit of generosity and fair-play which has heretofore characterized the relations between the two distinctive classes in this country, would quietly and easily effect a compromise where interests are so largely mutual.

The benefits of allotment are so manifest that an enumeration of them, except in a casual way, is unnecessary here. As matters stand now, tenants can negotiate no leases for a term of years; under allotment they could lease their farms and be fully protected in their rights by the courts. They have reclaimed this land from the wilderness by years of toil and expense, and caused it to blossom as the rose, but under the community system they cannot buy a foot of Indian soil; under allotment hundreds of non-citizens would buy farms of the tribal citizens, often on long time and easy terms, and a few years would equalize the ownership of land between the two races. The individualization of the land would also protect non-citizens in their residence in the nation. The tribal legislature has authority to regulate the permit system to suit itself. Annual permits have been twenty-five cents, twenty-five dollars and five dollars. The policy of the present administration is not liberal toward white settlers. Suppose it should raise the permit fee to an hundred dollars, or any sum restrictive in its effect? So long as the domain is held in common, the non-citizens would have to submit to such oppressive measures or be ejected as intruders. The opening of the country to capital and business, through a fixed land tenure, would also benefit the farmers by the creation of an excellent home market, for as the demand for their products is increased by an urban population, the supply and prices of these products must necessarily be increased. Under allotment the non-citizen farmer would not be subjected to oppressive legislation by the tribal government, in respect to the number of cattle he can hold.

From the citizen standpoint, the question is strikingly put thus: Would you prefer one-fourteen-thousandth interest in 9,000,000 acres of common land, to a warrantee deed from Uncle Sam to 600 acres? When you receive your patent, the question of your property rights is forever settled, and you know just what the future has in store for your children, so far as the tribal heritage is concerned. Is it not better to have this land individualized now, while the hearty co-operation of the federal government can be obtained, rather than trust to the uncertainty of the future? Politicians and governmental policies are the creatures of public opinion, whose fickle favor, with the Indian to-day, may be with his enemies to-morrow. Is it not possible that a few years may bring an administration that will utterly disregard treaties and bow to popular clamor for the Indian's land? Is there any certainty, in such an event, of the Chickasaw people being granted an equal division of tribal domain? These are questions for the dispassionate consideration of every citizen of this nation.

From the moment of issuance of patents, every acre of land in this country will begin a rapid ascent in value, and the citizen who wishes to dispose of a portion of his allotment can do so to advantage. The full-blood with his "tom-fuller" patch and log hut will awake to find himself a landlord in fact, and by making the best of his opportunities, can rapidly rise from poverty to wealth. Contact with the whites, under his changed relations, will beget assimilation, and his natural suspicion will be a safe-guard against white rapacity. He will demonstrate the fact that he can take care of himself. There are many crocodile tears shed for the full-blood, by the fellows who monopolize his interest in the land, when the subject of allotment is discussed. The theory of equality is chimerical among all races, conditions and times. Put 3,464 American citizens, selected indiscriminately from an agricultural community, upon the same acreage of land occupied by the Chickasaws, give each a patent to an equal share, and the disproportion of wealth would be as great, in a few years, as among the tribal citizens in the same time and under the same conditions.

In every human being there is an innate desire to have what is his own. As Agent Bennett said in one of his reports to the department, "allotment creates responsibility, individuality, and a desire to accumulate property; it teaches habits of industry and economy. A perfect and secure title to a man's possessions, will alone imbue his mind with ideas of true civilization." Allot the lands of the five civilized tribes, and the intruder question, which is now seriously threatening the peace of this country, and which may result in bloodshed, will be forever done away with; there will be no more bogus claimants to Indian citizenship; no more disputes among citizens over "claims."

The day has passed when citizens of the Indian Territory can be protected by an imaginary Chinese wall against white invasion. The day is passing when American citizens will be exiled as outlaws from petty sovereignties within the borders of the republic. Statesmen are beginning to regard Indian treaties from a practical, business standpoint, without splitting hairs on points of honor. The sacredness of such treaties is being classed with the false notion of the sacredness of precedent. What answered very well yesterday may not fill the requirements of to-day. As wise men change their opinions, so governments must change their policies to sui ie times. Congress must deal with the civilized tribal citizens of the Indian Territory as they are, not as their ancestors were in the early days of the republic, nor even as affairs were when the last treaties were made. The absurdity of governing a civilized people by the same intercourse laws which govern semi-barbarous, nomadic Indians, is too palpable for comment.

Higher than all individual interests, higher than the claims of tribal autonomy, are the demands of progress in the mighty young West. The Indian Territory lies directly in the pathway of commerce between the rapidly developing trans-Mississippi country and its Gulf outlet. A net-work of railroads is destined to traverse the length and breadth of the red man's land. Here will be built great cities, amply supported by the many industries to which this region is peculiarly adapted. Here will be developed the richest agricultural section in the Southwest. Few states in the union have such a diversity and abundance of natural resources. Here the fleecy staple of the south and the bearded grain of the north flourish on common soil. Rich in corn, kine and swine, the basis of the farmer's prosperity is already established. As a producer of coal, iron, lead, and perhaps more precious minerals, this country is destined to become famous. There are now 300,000 inhabitants in Oklahoma and the Indian Territory. With the opening of millions of new acres to white settlement, will come hundreds of thousands more. Within five years, it is not unreasonable to predict nearly a million people within the old bounds of the Indian Territory. In view of these facts, which must be apparent to all observing men, is it not the part of discretion for the Indian to have his lamp trimmed and burning for the coming of the bridegroom?

Chickasaw Laws.

AN ACT AUTHORIZING THE GOVERNOR TO GRANT PERMITS TO PERSONS WISHING TO TRADE IN THE CHICKASAW NATION.

WHEREAS, It is stipulated in the 39th Article of the Treaty of 1866, between the United States and the Choctaw and Chickasaw tribes of Indians, "That no person shall expose for sale in the country, any goods or other articles of merchandise, without obtaining a permit from the Legislature thereof;"

AND WHEREAS, The Legislature meets but once a year, which makes it difficult for traders, or other persons desiring to trade therein, to procure permits; therefore,

SEC. 1. Be it enacted by the Legislature of the Chickasaw Nation, That from and after the passage of this Act, the Governor is hereby authorized and empowered to grant permits to any respectable persons desiring to trade within the limits of the Chickasaw Nation; Provided, however, that the person or persons desiring to trade therein shall have five signers, citizens, before he, she or they can expose any goods or other articles of merchandise for sale or barter.

SEC. 2. Be it further enacted, That all persons in this Nation now and hereafter trading therein, under permit [citizens excepted], shall make, under oath, a true and correct statement to the Governor, of the amount of capital invested annually in goods or other articles of merchandise exposed for sale in this Nation, and shall pay to the Governor the sum of one per cent, annually, for said privileges, and the Governor shall report to the Auditor of Public Accounts quarterly, the number of permits given, and the amount collected by him from the persons obtaining permits under this Act, and the funds so collected shall be placed in the National Treasury, for National purposes.

SEC. 3. Be it further enacted, That if any persons, except citizens, shall expose any goods or articles or merchandise whatever for sale, without first obtaining a permit from the Governor, he shall incur the penalty of having all the goods and other articles of merchandise confiscated; the said confiscated property shall be sold by the Sheriff or Constable, at the county seat of the county where the said property has been seized, to the highest bidder, for cash or currency.

SEC. 4. Be it further enacted, That the said Sheriff or Constable shall report to the Auditor of Public Accounts, quarterly, the amount of property sold under the confiscating section of this Act; and he shall place the monies derived from the sale of all confiscated property, at the end of every fiscal quarter, in the National Treasury, to be applied to National purposes.

SEC. 5. Be it further enacted, That one per cent. shall be the rate of taxation charged by the Nation on all goods or merchandise, or other articles for sale or barter, to be paid to the Governor at the time the permit is given, and the said rate of taxation shall be charged and paid to the Governor for any and all goods, or other articles of merchandise or barter, which may be exposed for sale afterwards, on which the tax has not been paid; and any and all monies collected by the Governor, under the foregoing section of this Act, shall be reported to the Auditor of Public Accounts, and be placed in the National Treasury, for National purposes.

SEC. 6. Be it further enacted, That no permit shall be given under this Act for a longer period than three years; but the same may be renewed at the expiration of the time specified in the permit, in the same manner mentioned in the first section of this Act.

SEC. 7. Be it further enacted, That the length shall be limited—under three years—and specified in the permit, by which a person may trade in this Nation.

SEC. 8. Be it further enacted, That every citizen of this Nation, trading therein, exposing goods or other articles of merchandise for sale or barter, shall have a permit, but he shall be exempt from paying the taxes specified in this Act.

SEC. 9. Be it further enacted, That all laws and parts of laws conflicting with this Act are hereby declared to be null and void.

Approved, October 7, 1876, B. F. OVERTON,
Governor.

[NOTE: Some traders, in addition to their license from the tribal government, procure one from the United States, through the Union agency. Up to 1885 this course was necessary, but since then the United States has given the five civilized tribes the privilege of regulating their own licensed trader system, and a government license is now practically superfluous. The fee for taking out a U. S. license is simply for filling out the papers and administering the oath, the bond required being $10,000. In this connection traders should beware of outrageously extortionate fees exacted by unscrupulous officials, an instance of which has become notorious in Ardmore recently. The U. S. traders license is especially designed for traders on reservations occupied by blanket Indians, or tribes without a well regulated governmental system, and not for the Chickasaw, Choctaw, Cherokee, Creek snd Seminole nations. Some merchants reagard this license as an additional protection]—ED.

AN ACT DEFINING WHAT SHALL CONSTITUTE A CLAIM IN THE CHICKASAW NATION

SECTION 1. Be it enacted by the Legislature of the Chickasaw Nation, That a house out of either logs, plank or boards, not less than twelve feet square, fit for habitation, shall be a legal claim and hold good for twelve months; then every six months thereafter add one acre of land, prepared for cultivation, under a good and lawful fence until twenty acres have been taken in; then it shall be a lawful claim.

SEC. 2. Be it further enacted, That when any parent or guardian shall select a claim for his child or ward, he or she shall register the claim in the County Clerk's office of the county wherein the selection has been made, and fully comply with the provisions of the first section of this Act, shall be a legal and lawful claim.

SEC. 3. Be it further enacted, That when a place is registered for a child, that place cannot be sold or disposed of by the parent or guardian, except by the order of the County Court.

SEC. 4. Be it further enacted, That no parent or guardian shall select more than one place for each child, as provided in the second section of this Act.

SEC. 5. Be it further enacted, That when any citizen has abandoned any old place or claims shall renew them under the provision of the first section of this Act in six months, otherwise they shall revert and become public land of the Nation.

SEC. 6. Be it further enacted, That any citizen who shall abandon any claim for the period of two years it shall become public domain of the Nation, and subject to entry by any citizen of this Nation, any Act or part of Acts coming in conflict with the provisions of this Act be and the same is hereby repealed, and that this Act take effect from and after its passage. W. M. GUY,

APPROVED, September 24, 1887. Governor.

AN ACT TO INCORPORATE MINING COMPANIES IN THE CHICKASAW NATION.

SECTION 1. Be it enacted by the Legislature of the Chickasaw Nation, That any resident citizens (no less than three) of the Chickasaw Nation, who may wish to form a corporated company or companies to engage in developing coal mines, and to transport, ship or sell all coal mined beyond the limits of this Nation, shall be authorized to do so under the provisions hereinafter provided for by this Act.

SEC. 2. Be it further enacted, That when three or more citizens of this Nation form a corporative company to develop coal mines as provided for in the first section of this Act, shall first file a written application for a charter with the National Secretary designating the county and place, with the name of the company, and what the company wishes to develop and work, and file with the Governor a good and sufficient bond in the sum of ten thousand dollars ($10,000) payable to the Governor, and his successor in office, for the use and benefit of the Chickasaw Nation, for the faithful observance of the laws of the Nation, and to pay the tax on all coal mined or worked under the provisions of this Act; Provided further, the National Secretary shall issue to said company or companies a charter designating the location, places and county they propose to operate in, over his official signature, with the great seal of the Chickasaw Nation attached.

SEC. 3. Be it further enacted, That the company after complying with the provisions of this Act, shall have the authority to contract with capitalists to prospect for, develop and work coal mines as provided for in this Act, and to maintain and to operate the same, and to employ as much help as they may deem necessary to carry on their work, and shall pay the Permit Collector for all hands they may have in operating said mines.

SEC. 4. Be it further enacted, That the company or companies shall pay to the proper authority of the Chickasaw Nation, monthly one half cent per bushel on all coal mined.

SEC. 5. Be it further enacted, That the powers and priviliges conferred in this Act shall not operate to interfere with any individual claim or the right of any citizen, and provided further, should there be disputes arise as to the right of any claim, or suits arise for damages or for royalty the District Court shall appoint a receiver to hold the claim until the matter is adjusted and decided by the court as to whom it belongs.

SEC. 6. Be it further enacted, That the said co-operative company shall be allowed to build or cause to be built and operated such tramways as may be necessary to carry out the intent and meaning of this Act.

SEC. 7. Be it further enacted, That no charter shall be granted for a longer period than twenty years.

SEC. 8. Be it further enacted, That this Act shall include petroleum, natural gas and asphaltum, and the royalty on the same shall be two per cent. on all gross sales on each of said products.

SEC. 9. Be it further enacted, That the chartered coal companies in this nation shall have the privilege and right under their charter, to mine, operate and prospect for petroleum, asphaltum, [and] natural gas; Provided that the company shall first file notice with the National Secretary of their intention in writing, then the National Secretary shall certify the fact on the back of the application for their charter, then give the company a certificate of his endorsement on the application, and include in said certificate that said company had the right to prospect for, and operate for either petroleum, asphaltum and natural gas, export and sell the same by paying the royalty to the Nation as provided for in the eighth Section of this Act.

SEC. 10. Be it further enacted, That the company shall have the right to, and build oil tanks and lay pipe lines to convey petroleum and natural gas to market, and to operate the same to enable them to successfully carry on their business.

SEC. 11. Be it further enacted, That this Act shall include iron ore, and the royalty due and belonging to the Chickasaw Nation on iron ore shall be one-half of a cent per ton on all gross sales and shipments of the same in its crude state, and the said royalty shall be paid in like manner as that on coal, petroleum, asphaltum and natural gas; and companies to develop and work the said iron ore or any other minerals, may be formed, organized and chartered, as authorized by the said Acts governing the above named products, and said companies shall comply with all the requirements of the said Acts governing the development and mining of coal, petroleum, asphaltum and natural gas, and be governed by the same [laws] as herein provided, and said charter may be issued for the same period of time.

SEC. 12. Be it further enacted, That all Acts or parts of Acts coming in conflict with the provisions of this Act, be and they are hereby repealed, and this Act take effect and be in full force from and after its passage.

APPROVED, December 21, 1886. WM. M. GUY, Governor.

AN ACT IN RELATION TO STOCK UNLAWFULLY RANGING AND GRAZING IN THE CHICKASAW NATION.

WHEREAS, The United States Government has pledged the Chickasaw Nation protection from the intrusion of cattle and cattlemen, and as it is a very difficult matter to control this class of intrusion;

AND WHEREAS, All efforts to remove and collect penalties for such intrusion have been attended with an outlay as large, if not larger, than the collections therefrom;

AND WHEREAS, We should not call for aid or protection until we are unable to protect ourselves;

AND WHEREAS, Our protests for years have been in vain against this intrusion, and in spite of our protests and the aid of the United States Government in the expulsion of this class of intrusion, it still exists in violation of the Intercourse Laws and of our laws, trampling alike on our rights and our domain, Therefore,

SECTION 1. Be it enacted by the Legislature of the Chickasaw Nation, That no cattle or stock of any kind belonging to non-citizens shall be permitted to range or graze within the limits of the Chickasaw Nation, unless so permitted for farmers under the provisions of the permit law, and any cattle or stock found so ranging, or grazing shall be taken up by the Stock Superintendent, one of whom shall be appointed in each county, whose office is hereby created, or by persons under his employment and they shall be kept under herd for the period of thirty days unless before the expiration of the thirty days, the owner thereof shall appear and properly identify the same.

SEC. 2. Be it further enacted, That if before the expiration of thirty days after such stock of non-citizens has been taken up the owner shall appear and identify them he shall upon the payment of one dollar per head be permitted to take possession of said stock and drive them from within the limits of the Chickasaw Nation, and if after the expiration of thirty days after identification said stock are not so driven out the Superintendent shall again take possession of them and hold them until payment of one dollar per head as before, and so on until all the stock shall be removed, one-half of the money so collected shall be retained by the Superintendent; and the balance shall be turned over to the National Treasurer for National purposes, and the Superintendent shall be required to make his reports quarterly to the Governor and Auditor.

SEC. 3. Be it further enacted, That if at the expiration of thirty days after the stock of non-citizens has been taken up by the Superintendent, the owner or owners thereof shall not have appeared and identified said stock, the Superintendent shall after public advertisement, describing said cattle or stock by kinds, marks and brands in at least three public places in the Chickasaw Nation, to be posted at least fifteen days, dispose of said stock or so much thereof as will pay the one dollar per head, at public sale to the highest bidder for cash, one-half of the proceeds of such sale to be retained by the Superintendent, the balance to be turned over to the National Treasurer for National purposes.

SEC. 4. Be it further enacted, That for the purpose of carrying out the provisions of this Act and for such other purposes as may be hereafter provided, the Governor shall appoint some competent person to serve as Superintendent until the convening of the Legislature in September 1888, at which time there shall be Superintendents elected by a joint vote of both Houses of the Legislature, who shall hold their office for the term of two years, the Superintendent so appointed or elected shall be required to take the usual oath of office and he shall be required to give bond for the faithful performance of the duties of his office; said bond shall be for twenty-five hundred dollars to be made payable to the Governor of the Chickasaw Nation, and shall be approved by the Governor of the Chickasaw Nation, and having filled such bond and taken such oath the District Judge shall certify the same to the Governor, upon which the Governor shall grant the Superintendent his commission.

SEC. 5. Be it further enacted, [That] the Superintendent shall be permitted to employ as deputies such citizens of the Chickasaw Nation as in his judgment may be required, and each deputy shall be required to take an oath for the faithful performance of his duties, which oath may be administered by any qualified Judge of the Chickasaw Nation, and said deputies shall be paid by the Superintendent for their services.

SEC. 6. Be it further enacted, That the Superintendent shall defray all expenses incurred, in collecting said one dollar per head on cattle or stock found unlawfully ranging or grazing in the Chickasaw Nation, and shall render annually his report to the Legislature.

SEC. 7. Be it further enacted, That it is hereby made the duty of each County Clerk of this Nation to furnish said Superintendent a certified list of all marks and brands recorded in their counties and the Superintendent shall keep a record of all marks and brands of citizens of this Nation in his office, and that this Act take effect and be in force from and after its passage.

APPROVED, October 14, 1886. WM. M. GUY,
Governor.

AN ACT TO PROHIBIT LEASING LAND.

SECTION 1. Be it enacted by the Legislature of the Chickasaw Nation, That from and after the passage of this Act, the leasing of land is hereby prohibited within the limits of this Nation, and every citizen violating this Act shall be fined in any sum not exceeding one thousand dollars, at the discretion of the District Court having jurisdiction; and the lease shall be adjudged to be void from the beginning, and the lessee shall be removed from beyond the limits of the Chickasaw Nation, by the Sheriff or Constable of the county where the lease was made, or the lessee or lessees, as the case may be.

SEC. 2. Be it further enacted, That the foregoing section shall not be construed to interfere with or invalidate leases entered into before the passage of this Act, nor to interfere with or prohibit citizens from renting their places for a term not exceeding a year, as practiced heretofore; and that the fines collected under the provisious of this Act shall be placed in the National Treasury, for National purposes.

APPROVED, October 10, 1876. B. F. OVERTON, Governor.

AN ACT PROHIBITING CITIZENS FROM HOLDING STOCK FOR NON-CITIZENS.

SECTION 1. Be it enacted by the Legislature of the Chickasaw Nation, That from and after the passage of this Act, no citizens, or person under permit, shall hold for pasturage in this Nation, any stock of any kind, in his name or otherwise, belonging to non-citizens.

SEC. 2. Be it further enacted, That any person reported for violation of the first Section of this Act, to the County Judge, shall be taken before said Judge, who shall investigate the case, and if, upon the evidence of one or more witnesses, the accused be found guilty, the Judge shall remand him for further trial to the District Court, and report the non-citizen, the owner of said stock, to the Governor, who shall report him to the United States Agent, and ask of said agent the application of the Intercourse law for pasturing stock.

SEC. 3. Be it further enacted, That the District Court shall, after a verdict of conviction, fine the citizen so offending not less than one hundred dollars, nor more than five hundred dollars; this fine to be collected as other fines, one-half to go to the informant, the other into the County Treasury, for county purposes; and if not able to pay the fine imposed, the offender shall be lodged in the National Jail for a period of not less than two nor more than six months, at the discretion of the court.

APPROVED, October, 17, 1876. B. F. OVERTON, Governor.

AN ACT IN RELATION TO ESTRAYS.

SECTION 1. Be it enacted by the Legislature of the Chickasaw Nation, That from and after the passage of this Act, all strays running with the property of any citizen of this Nation, the owner of which is not known, shall be taken up, and a description of said stock, in writing, posted at the court ground of each county for three months; after which time, if no owner appears, then the taker up of such stray or strays shall be required to take said stock before the County Judge of the county in which he may live; then it shall be the duty of the Judge to authorize two or more persons to appraise the same, and the description and value taken down in writing by the appraisers, which description and value shall be furnished the County Clerk. Then it shall be the duty of the County Clerk to advertise the same in three or more public places in his county, and if the owner does not appear within twelve months, the property shall be sold to the highest bidder by the Sheriff or Constable of the county, by the Clerk first giving fifteen days' notice of the time and place the sale is to take place; and one half the proceeds of said sale or sales shall go to the taker up, upon his paying the County Clerk one dollar and fifty cents, and the other half shall go into the County Treasury for county purposes.

SEC. 2. Be it further enacted, That all stray cattle, horses, mules, jacks or jennets, taken up by any person, shall be posted and sold, and the proceeds divided as defined in section first of this Act, but should the owner appear before the expiration of the twelve months, and prove his or her property, before any Judge, he or she shall be entitled to the same, by paying one dollar and fifty cents per head each to the Clerk and taker up.

SEC. 3. Be it further enacted, That sheep, hogs and goats shall be dealt with in the same manner as other stray stock, with this exception: that if the owner should appear before any Judge and prove them, before the expiration of the twelve months, he or she shall be entitled to the same, by paying fifty cents per head each to the Clerk and taker up.

SEC. 4. Be it further enacted, That when any person having strays running in his range, and fails to post them, the County Judge shall direct the Sheriff or Constable to take charge of such strays and cause them to be posted and put in possession of any other person within his county.

SEC. 5. Be it further enacted, That any person or persons having taken up any stray or strays, and shall abuse or disfigure them in any way, shall be subject to a fine of not less than five nor exceeding ten dollars, when convicted by the County Court that the offender lives in. The County Judge shall cause said fine to be collected, and when collected shall go to the owner of said property so disfigured or abused. But should the owner or owners of said property be unknown, then the said fine shall be put into the County Treasury for county purposes, and the County Judge shall order any Sheriff or Constable to take any property that the said person or persons (so disfiguring strays) may have, and sell to the highest bidder, by first giving fifteen days' notice at one or more places in his county.

SEC. 6. Be it further enacted, That whenever any Sheriff or Constable sells any stray stock under the provisions of this Act, he shall give to the purchaser a bill of sale, in the name of the Chickasaw Nation, of such stock sold by him; said bill of sale to be recorded in the County Clerk's office, and the same shall be valid to all intents and purposes.

APPROVED, October 7, 1876. B. F. OVERTON,
Governor.

DATE DUE

86473			